how to start a home-based

Massage Therapy Business

Shirley L. Philbrick, LMT

g**pp**®

Guilford, Connecticut

To buy books in quantity for corporate use
or incentives, call **(800) 962-0973**
or e-mail **premiums@GlobePequot.com.**

Interior spot art licensed by Shutterstock.com
Art on pp. 125, 128, and 132 by Lori Enik

Editorial Director: Cynthia Hughes Cullen
Editor: Tracee Williams
Project Editor: Lauren Brancato
Text Design: Sheryl P. Kober
Layout: Sue Murray

Library of Congress Cataloging-in-Publication Data is available on file.

ISBN 978-0-7627-7204-9

Printed in the United States of America

10 9 8 7 6 5 4 3 2 1

This book's purpose is to provide accurate and authoritative information on the topics covered.
It is sold with the understanding that neither the author nor the publisher is engaged in render-
ing legal, financial, accounting, and other professional services. Neither Globe Pequot Press nor
the author assumes any liability resulting from action taken based on the information included
herein. Mention of a company name does not constitute endorsement.

The health information expressed in this book is based solely on the personal experience of the
author and is not intended as a medical manual. The information should not be used for diagnosis or treatment, or as a substitute for professional medical care.

To the human spirit in all of us that strives to reach ever higher.

Contents

Acknowledgments

Special thanks to my daughter, Brittany, who has stood by me patiently and lovingly through *mi vida loca,* all the while saying with the utmost confidence, "Mom, you can do this," and to my stepdaughter, Kristy, who not only shares my passion for the written word but also knows the rigors of the writer's life. I am honored to share the path, and I feel blessed to have you both.

Much appreciation goes out to friends, clients, colleagues, and family who have taught me so much about the dual professions I've chosen. Each shares a deep and abiding faith in me that encourages me to focus and believe when I need the reminder most. Your support and wisdom are nothing short of amazing.

To my former massage therapy instructor, Donna Kraft-Smith, I offer deepest gratitude for not only teaching, but demonstrating, the invaluable lesson that massage is a dance—one performed not only with technical skill and strength of mind, body, and spirit, but also with compassion, kindness, and grace.

For my editor, Tracee, who found me through my online writing and has assisted me most graciously throughout the process of writing this book, thank you for your patience, expertise, and, most importantly, for giving me the opportunity to share what I know.

And finally, I extend sincere thanks to Jeff for pushing me out of the nest so hard I thought I'd break a wing but, incredibly, learned to fly instead.

Introduction

You picked up this book for a reason. Maybe you're exploring home-based business options or you're a massage therapy student with a desire to operate your practice from home. It's even possible that you're a seasoned professional looking for some ways to work more efficiently, make more money, or even just liven up a tired practice.

Whatever walk of life you're from, if the massage therapy field is on your path, you will find my book to be a practical source of information, interspersed with humor, tips, and ideas that come from someone who's done it. I have been where you are, or where you're headed. The road has bumps and a lot of potholes, but it also has the thrill of reaching the goals you set for yourself and the success that accompanies it.

My own massage journey began many years ago when I saw a tiny one-inch advertisement in the local paper for a massage therapy training program. I clipped the ad out of the paper and stuck it on my refrigerator where it stayed for nearly two years until the paper yellowed and the words faded. I eventually threw the paper away, but never the thought of becoming a massage therapist.

I began to study my options and discovered that training programs in my state were limited and would include extensive daily travel or the need for overnight lodging, which was neither affordable nor conducive to caring for my family. But before long another classified ad appeared in the newspaper and I took this one as a sign of what I was meant to do. The ad was for a relatively new massage-therapy training program that was in my local area, where I could attend full-day classes on weekends.

My next hurdle after finding a school came when I interviewed with the school's instructor. The cost was far out of reach for me at that point in my life. But the idea of becoming an LMT (licensed massage therapist) would not be put to rest, so I took several part-time jobs to pay my monthly tuition. The work was physically demanding but it afforded me not only the income to pay tuition without taking out loans, but also the flexibility of schedule to take care of my family and still be able to study, take exams, and practice my massage therapy skills on people who volunteered to let me work on them. Note that there is never a lack of volunteers to willingly lend a hand or, in this case, a body for massage practice sessions. Sometimes, however, it becomes difficult to convert non-paying practice clients into paying clients once you are fully trained and licensed. I was fortunate and am forever grateful to the wonderful people I worked for and the many others who were my practice clients and eventually became long-term paying clients.

In approximately eighteen months, I had a massage therapy license in hand and more excitement inside me than I could possibly contain. Yet when I walked away from school after graduating, I learned very quickly that clients didn't magically schedule themselves in the brand-new day planner I received as a graduation gift!

Although I'd had some business training in school and obtained several paying clients from my tenure as a student, I was ill-prepared for dealing with the process of getting a steady flow of massage clients to call and come in on a regular basis. In fact, "sporadic" was the name of the game when I first started my practice. Put the word "very" with sporadic and that aptly described the new endeavor I was so excited to embark on. That first year was an eye-opening experience. Here I was, full of energy, enthusiasm, and well-trained in the theory and practice of therapeutic massage. I knew I could help people and I was impatient to do just that. But the clientele I got were mostly the people I had known as a student and they were already familiar with my work. The biggest and least expensive marketing technique I knew of was word-of-mouth advertising, so I offered incentives to those few clients to encourage them to send business my way. It helped some, but not enough to create the boom I had hoped for. Frustration and a moderate degree of worry set in by the end of that first year in business.

I knew that what I was doing wasn't working and it was time for a change in plan. Oh, that's right I didn't *have* a plan. So for me it took a combination of my massage education and a tremendous amount of trial and error, but I learned a lot about owning and operating a home-based massage therapy practice. I listened when clients told me not to put on the "perpetual sale" (meaning continual discounts) because people would only want to come to me if I was having a sale. I took heed when a client wisely said, "If you don't manage your time, other people will," in reference to my days and times of operation. I studied new creative ways of marketing, I consulted with other service professionals in my area, and I talked to local LMTs to find out what they were doing to gain clients. I educated myself about the barter system and found out that in many areas (especially rural) it is a very common means of doing business. I learned quite quickly that though it was an interesting concept—this idea of trading yard work, chickens, and haircuts for massage therapy services—it didn't pay the expenses of owning and operating a business. I learned a tremendous amount about the business world in those early days. I continue that learning process and the fine-tuning of my skills both as a practitioner and as a business owner to this day.

Interspersed throughout the body of this book, you will read several "Real-Life Stories" that are actual tales or lessons learned from my own massage-therapy business-building experience. There are far too many more to list in one manuscript and yet I share a few so you can connect with me in a more real way and realize that I have "walked the walk" just as you have, or will.

My suggestion to you, the reader, is don't just read the book and put it on the shelf with the others. Implement the ideas and concepts that best suit your situation and the massage-therapy business you wish to build. Learning from others who have done what you are setting out to do and tailoring that knowledge to suit your own needs is an integral part of making any business work. So I encourage you to use this book for the reasons it was written: to sharpen your own skills, stimulate your

Real-Life Story

I once scheduled a client two hours earlier than my usual 9 a.m. start. I didn't set my alarm as my internal one usually wakes me in more than enough time to prepare for work. That morning, it failed. I woke, startled, fifteen minutes prior to when the client was due to arrive. I jumped out of bed and into my clothes. I brushed my hair and teeth and hastily applied some makeup. I had five minutes to spare to grab a glass of orange juice and turn on the massage music before she arrived. THAT'S the difference between working at home and working away from home.

creative mind, and ultimately, assist you on your journey to a wildly successful home-based massage therapy business. Take note that as you delve into the book, you'll find that many concepts are repeated in other areas, and at the end of each chapter is a final section that reviews its main points. Heed these messages for their importance and realize that they bear repeating for the valuable insights they contain.

In closing, I would say this to you: Envision what you want so clearly that you can see, smell, taste, hear, and touch it. Do this repeatedly and then follow the actions you are inspired to take. Once you do, having what you desire will follow.

01 Home Massage Therapy Business Pros and Cons

Starting your own business, no matter the type, requires forethought and a definitive plan of action. Perhaps most importantly are the concepts of a "can-do" mind-set and follow-through of action. Ultimately, if you know in your mind that you can succeed and you plan accordingly, you will find or make the opportunities to bring about that success. Planning is essential yet it's inspired action that will take you where you want to go. Essentially, if all you do is think about your business (the fun part) and stay in planning mode, you will not find the success you seek and deserve.

And as with all home-based businesses, there are advantages and disadvantages to working for yourself. It's important to weigh these out carefully and address how they may affect your massage therapy practice. Finding out why you want to build your own home-based business and the pros and cons of doing so is an important part of establishing that business. This knowledge could be considered an essential part of the foundation for all that will come after.

Advantages

The advantages to working for yourself are numerous. From financial considerations to sheer convenience, there are more than enough reasons to at least consider the idea. Thinking of all the pros to owning and operating a business helps motivate you and is just plain fun to think about! Be advised though that all things have a flip side and the advantages of having a home-based massage therapy business are no exception to that rule.

1. **Money.** An obvious advantage is saving costs. Having a home-based practice significantly reduces the expense of maintaining an office

location. Though you may have a home mortgage, you won't have the additional rent or lease costs that are typically the major expense for a massage practitioner. In a nutshell, because you work for yourself at home, you keep what you earn instead of giving a substantial percentage to a landlord, spa, or other facility that massage therapists often work in.

2. **Travel.** Working from home saves money on gas, wear and tear on your vehicle, and the time spent commuting back and forth. The time saved may allow for completion of other projects in the home that would normally be saved for weekends and evenings with a traditional job.

3. **Hours of operation.** A home-based massage business may afford you the opportunity to work around other jobs or family schedules and obligations. This is a perk you won't get by working for someone else.

4. **Who's the boss?** YOU ARE. You set your hours, fees, determine policies, and choose the type of clients you want to work with. The good news is you can't be fired or laid off.

5. **Tax advantages.** You are able to deduct at least a portion of your home and business expenses like massage business-related travel, office-equipment purchases, and utility or other home- and health-related costs. This can be an invaluable plus to having a home-based practice.

Disadvantages

As mentioned earlier, because everything created has its opposite, so, too, does the home-based massage business have its disadvantages. It's common to be so excited by the prospects of starting a business that one focuses on the advantages and overlooks the disadvantages. Being optimistic is ideal but having your own business takes a healthy dose of reality too. Create balance between the two as you explore your new business's potential and your own personal potential to be a business owner.

1. **Separation issues.** The massage space optimally should be segregated from personal living space. This is difficult to achieve in the average home unless you have a dedicated room available that will be used exclusively for massage. The basic fact is, no matter how well presented your home is, it is still a home and does not lend to a strong professional image the way commercial property can. Making the appearance as professional as possible and keeping

the business space as a separate entity from personal living space whenever possible is ideal.

2. **Cleanliness.** If a client has to enter your home to access the massage space, your house must be kept neat and clean all the time. This is a more obvious drawback for those who do not clean or pick up daily. However, a plus to the home-based business is there may be available time in between clients to keep things tidied up. Hiring a housekeeper once a week to do the major cleaning and delegating chores throughout the week to family members may be an optimal solution to what could present a problem in retaining clientele.

3. **Pets and kids.** If animals and other people must be in the home during working hours, noise may be a distraction. Pet odor and allergens may also be a deterring factor. Being able to separate family from business can be difficult with a home-based practice. Young children may need to be put in day care and pets in seclusion during business hours. This may incur extra expense or inconvenience.

4. **Isolation.** Working in a home-based business is typically very solitary. Most clients prefer a quiet, relaxing environment so conversation is often limited to before and after sessions. If you like to converse and be around groups of people on a regular basis, you will need to find other avenues outside the work environment to fulfill those needs. Consider joining a networking group that meets once or twice a month to discuss business ideas, participating in workshops, associating with other colleagues, or taking a night class. Spend time with friends and family and be sure to get out of the house every day at some point, even if it's for a walk around the neighborhood.

5. **Undesirables.** As a massage therapist you will inevitably encounter the new, unknown person who turns out to be someone you don't want as a client, let alone to know where you live. This may be someone who presents a possible danger or simply makes you feel uncomfortable through words or actions. For this reason many massage therapists will only take clients referred by someone they know. This is not always possible, however, so an awareness that working from home has an inherent risk factor is important. Using a separate business phone line and post office box, as well as learning how to effectively screen potential clients over the phone before seeing them in your office, will assist with safety concerns.

What Qualities and Skills Do I Have?

Take the time to go through the ten self-evaluation questions found below and have a heart-to-heart talk with yourself about each one. Be honest and take note of what traits you have that will enhance your home-based massage business and those that have been, or could be, jeopardizing your chances at success. Acknowledging your traits should never be construed as a put-down of yourself. It's simply an assessment of your innate qualities and learned skills that may be helpful, or not, to your chosen endeavor of having a home-based business. The self-assessment is important to the start of any business and should be repeated from time to time to stay on the fast track to success.

Once you've completed your own self-evaluation, read the next section on "What Qualities and Skills Do I Need?" to further your understanding of the importance of each question.

What Qualities and Skills Do I Need?

If you answered the questions below as truthfully as possible, you now have a good idea of your areas of strength and weakness. Each bullet point on the following page will ask you to question yourself in more depth. Deepen your understanding of the concepts presented, as they explain why each point is paramount to the success of

Self-Evaluation Quiz

1. How do I relate to people?
2. Do I see every body as acceptable?
3. Am I self-motivated?
4. At what level are my organizational skills?
5. Am I committed?
6. How is my physical health?
7. Where do I see my business in six months, a year, or five years?
8. How do I balance work and play?
9. Does my family support me in having a home-based business?
10. Am I willing to work other hours beyond the traditional nine-to-five workday?

your home-based massage therapy business. As you note each one, rate where you think you would score on a 1 to 5 scale, with 1 being poor and 5 being excellent. Once you've finished it will then be possible to see where you need to hone your skills and in which areas you are proficient.

- **Interpersonal skills.** For starters, do you like being around and interacting with others? Let's face it, there are fewer more intimate settings than a one-on-one massage therapy session between you and another person. Empathy, excellent listening skills, compassion, humor, cheerfulness, and a host of other people skills are essential. People will naturally come to you in pain, sometimes with illnesses, needing stress relief, or simply desiring to be pampered. They want, and will expect, a massage practitioner who will give adequate attention to them and their needs in return for the fee they pay. Every single day, no matter what is going on in your personal or business life, clients will come to you with needs to be met. Because they are paying for your massage therapy services, they have every right to expect you to leave your own troubles outside the massage room door and devote the session time to them. A client is not there to hear about how your dog ran away or your child was sick all night and you didn't get any sleep. You, as the practitioner, are obligated to put a smile on your face, listen to your client, and provide, to the best of your ability, a massage session to address their needs.

- **Every body acceptance.** I don't mean everybody, I mean every *body*. Contrary to what a new practitioner sees in pictures on brochures and in textbooks, not every body you see is equipped with six-pack abs and smooth, soft skin. If excess body hair or weight, wrinkles and sags, warts, bad breath, and cellulite thighs are just not for you, likely neither is the massage therapy business. Bodies come in all shapes, sizes, colors, and conditions. Most students, and certainly seasoned practitioners, have seen many body types, but if you are considering the profession for the very first time to see if it's a fit for you, then realizing that none of us is perfect is one of the first lessons to learn. If you can unconditionally accept the perfectly imperfect bodies you'll see, keep reading. If you can't, you can probably close this book now.

- **Self-motivation.** You're the boss. This means no one else is going to plan your business or your workday for you. Can you realistically take on the responsibilities that come with owning and operating a home-based massage therapy business? It's certainly comforting to know that you can't get fired for not doing your accounting last night because you had late clients and were tired, but remember, you and only you are the key to your success day to day, month to month, and year to year. Unless you hire it out, you are the marketer, the record keeper, the accounts payable and receivable departments, the housekeeper, and, of course, the massage therapist. That's a lot of hats to wear on top of those roles you may already have as a spouse, parent, or homeowner. Are you ready to take all that responsibility on yourself?

- **Matters of organization.** Honestly critique yourself in this area, taking a hard look at how you personally care for yourself, the typical daily condition of your home, your personal financial management, how well you balance work and family obligations, and maybe most importantly, what you accomplish by the end of each day. Many people are surprised at day's end to find that they completed very little of what they thought or set out to do that morning. Getting waylaid by phone calls, e-mail, text messages, chores, and other distractions can severely alter productivity in any home-based business operation and, unfortunately, is a very easy trap that the home worker can fall into. To-do lists may be a thing of the past with cell phones and other digital devices to keep us organized, but sometimes a simple sticky note with a list of things to accomplish and the time frame for each can do wonders for the perennially unproductive. Be sure to check them off and give yourself praise for each item completed. Keep in mind that to-do lists are never-ending. Don't let this discourage you.

- **Your health.** Massage therapy is a health-care profession. In order to educate and convince clients of the benefits of massage and other healthy-living options, you as the practitioner must show by example as well as tell. The rigors of performing massage therapy in conjunction with attending to the other, equally important, details of operating a business and home life require plenty of energy and stamina. Ergonomics, movement, and posture are all important to anyone doing the same type of repetitive workday in and day out. Continually assessing your own risk for injury and maintaining a moderate degree of overall mental and physical fitness is crucial to sustaining your practice day in and day out.

- **Commitment and determination.** Ask yourself if you have the discipline to do what it takes to run your own business. Is your attitude "can-do" or "I think so"? Will you throw in the towel if it gets too difficult or don't make six figures your first year in practice? Can you commit to promoting your business through weekly marketing practices, managing your finances, and furthering your education in the massage field on a regular basis? Many massage therapists despise the very thought of bookkeeping and promoting their practice but it's part of the job description unless, again, you choose to hire someone to do it for you. New and seasoned practitioners alike may have limited resources to pay professionals to do these types of jobs and thus must do them themselves to be successful. Ask yourself if you are committed enough to accurately attend to these more tedious aspects of running a business every day. A firm level of commitment is not a maybe; it's a must if you want your business to not only survive but thrive.

- **Business vision.** Close your eyes and envision what your massage practice will look like in six months, a year, or even five years down the road. Start by asking why you're in the business you're in. Likely your answer is to help people. What does this look like for you specifically? Do you see yourself choosing a massage specialization? Do you want to subcontract to other massage therapists or sell products? What amount of money do you project yourself making? What excites you when you see it in your mind's eye? Always see the possibilities in your business future. Taking it day to day is a common mistake that a massage therapist, new or seasoned, might make. Setting your future business vision can also assist you in preparing for eventualities like what you'll do if you need or want to take personal time off, or what plans you'll make to fill cancellation or no-show client sessions.

- **Staying balanced.** Maybe you're a hard worker and know how to put in long hours. Do you also know how to put work aside for play? Balance is essential in a profession that is very caregiver oriented. All work and no play not only makes Jack (or Jill) dull, but nothing will burn out a massage therapist faster, leaving them ready to give up their hard-earned practice. Another common exclamation from massage therapists is "My work IS my play!" To find a career you feel blessed every day to be a part of is what most of us wait our whole lives for, but you likely have friends and family, hobbies, and activities you're interested in also. Don't let them go by the wayside as you focus all your energy and time in your business. Enjoy your work by all means, but participate in hobbies, family vacations, and other activities to round out your life.

- **Family support.** Is your family behind you all the way in your quest for a home-based business? If not, in all honesty, you've got a hard road ahead. Operating any business from home means everyone makes concessions (i.e., noise reduction, helping you keep the house clean, and possibly leaving when clients are there). They may have to put up with you working longer or odd hours. Often when clients are done coming for the day, family members may think this means you're done working for the day. You may still have client notes to write or type up, or bookkeeping and cleaning to do yet. The "after-client" work involved in running a massage therapy business is often the very piece that family members overlook and may become frustrated by. Work together to see how you can make your dream of a home-based business a reality, while still allowing home to be home for everyone else.
- **Setting hours.** To be totally truthful, if you're seeing nine-to-five business hours in your future, your income levels will show it. What does that mean? It means a good portion of people you will have for clients also work. If they're working the same or similar hours as you, they don't always have the ability to leave work to come for massage. This means accommodating them with some evening or weekend hours. (Note: For those who do massage as a hobby or for part-time income, working typical day hours may work out just fine.) With that said, you still need to set boundaries for your work-related hours. If you allow your clients to "set" your hours based on their own personal schedules, you may find yourself asked to work on major holidays such

---

Real-Life Story

In the first years of my practice, I did on-site massage work in addition to having a home office. I worked at many of my on-site locations in the early evenings and weekends. As time passed, people asked for more and more of my time. Once I was asked if I could start doing a client's massage sessions at 9 or 10 p.m. so he could just go to bed afterward. Other times I've been asked to provide massage on Christmas Day, Easter Sunday, or Thanksgiving. A client who owned her own business wisely counseled me to set boundaries or someone else would be happy to set them for me.

as Christmas, on Sundays (which you may be fine with), or in the late hours of the night—none of which may be conducive to operating a home-based business with a family.

What Are Your Motivating Factors?

The biggest advantage of a home-based massage business is saving time and money on travel and business overhead, in addition to tax deductions. Renting or leasing massage space alone can cost thousands of dollars per year, on top of a home mortgage if you have one. This alone can become a substantial deciding factor in whether or not to operate from home. Add to this the possible cost of utilities, and a home-based practice may be the optimal choice for many—especially new practitioners just starting out.

The convenience of walking from one part of your house to another to go to work is irrefutable as well, particularly for those who live in wintry climates or densely populated areas where travel and commute times are extensive. However convenient working from home may be, you are, at times, going to have strangers in your home and you must accept that basic fact. Having safety measures in place is important, as well as working out a routine for your family so harmony can exist between work life and home life. This can be an obvious challenge for many practitioners.

Proper preparations to ready your home space (including the yard) for clients is essential to attend to on a regular basis. Safety and sanitation in your home working environment are crucial not only to reduce business liability risks, but also to safeguard your personal assets through preventative measures lest a client become injured on your property. Remember that most massage therapists are sole proprietors and therefore bear all the burden of responsibility when it comes to issues of liability. Being prepared will lessen the risks involved considerably.

Beyond the basic massage therapy skills you have or will learn in a training program, you will also need to be committed to your personal health and that of your business; have good-to-excellent organizational skills; be accepting of a wide range of body types and conditions; and be able to relate well to people. You must be your own boss and, at times, a cheerleader, and discipline and motivate yourself even on the bad days when you've had two no-shows, the dog ate your newspaper, and you have a headache from lack of sleep. Periodically assessing these skills and qualities in yourself is a good habit to get into to increase the odds of success for your home-based business.

02

Imagine the Possibilities

So here you are with sticky notes all over your desk, covered with ideas on what you want your dream business to look like. You're excited, you're confident, and you're ready to go full steam ahead. You've certainly considered the advantages, and likely to a lesser extent, the disadvantages, and you're impatient to press onward.

Yet somewhere between the ideas that keep you sleepless at night and the actual construction of this home-based business you've so clearly pictured is the hard work of research and development. This is the part where you do your homework to see if this idea you've had brewing is even feasible. State and local regulations may make your choices for you, depending on how stringent they are in your area. This is the time to ask for assistance from those in a more knowledgeable position to help you with regulatory or legal matters concerning a home-based business start-up. It's also the time to zero in on the more specific details. You'll need to know the genre of client you plan to see, whether you'll do all in-office massage, outcall, or try to combine the two, what type of massage you will employ, and the intricacies of planning out your massage office space.

Any business takes sufficient planning and research. A home-based option requires a unique approach, as it combines personal and business and, as I've stated before, it's not as simple as hanging a shingle that says, "Open for Business."

Permits and Zoning

Know the permit and zoning laws for your state, county, town, or city. Some have no, or few, restrictions and others may make it seemingly impossible to do business in your area. If you're a new practitioner or one looking for a change of location, check out local and state laws before opening for business in your home.

One mistake that a new massage therapist may make is confusing a massage license with a business license. A massage license is a license to practice that profession in your state. A business license is a separate entity that may be required to operate any type of business. Not all areas require a business license, but many will so it's important to find out.

Beyond the business license is a Doing Business As, or DBA. The DBA is a fictitious name for your business if you choose to use one. You must file a DBA with your county or state to make sure that no one else is using the same name for

Local Ordinances

From state to state, county to county, and city to city laws, ordinances, and regulations vary a great deal. One town may have no governing regulations regarding a massage therapy business yet the town or city five miles down the road may have very strict regulations.

As an example, one small town in rural Maine has a lengthy ordinance governing massage therapy business practices within the town limits. This ordinance was designed to prevent sexual acts or paid sexual services under the guise of a legitimate therapeutic massage and bodywork practice. Its regulations include, but aren't limited to, requiring a business license as well as a massage therapy practitioner license; a $500 annual application fee submitted to the town clerk; regular health, fire, and safety inspections; as well as practitioner criminal background checks. Any violations to the ordinance may result in loss of business licensure or hefty fines. This in-depth, and costly, type of ordinance may be a deal breaker for some massage therapists or those people thinking of getting into or starting this sort of business.

In other locales, zoning laws may restrict operating a business in one zone, yet allow it in another zone within the same city limits. Setting up a massage therapy business without checking on zoning and other governing regulations within any city or town is a serious mistake that can not only result in a significant loss of money but also the closure of your business.

their business. Many massage practitioners will use their own name (i.e., Jane Doe Massage Therapy) for ease, but others may wish to make up a business name (i.e., Dragonfly Serenity Massage Therapy) to create their own unique business identity. Registering your DBA helps ensure that no one else uses your business name.

Home-based businesses are not exempt from zoning or permit laws. Many areas have laws specifically to regulate where home-based businesses may be located and how they may operate. Other permits required may include a seller's certificate if you intend to sell products, a DBA permit, and possibly a permit from public health and safety or police departments.

Most state massage licensing boards will provide all the information a practitioner will need to start up a home-based massage business in their location. You can also contact your city hall or the county clerk's office for more information on doing business in your area.

Your Business Structure

So what will it be? Deciding your legal business structure is something you'll have to do sooner rather than later, though many massage practitioners operate as sole proprietors for the life of their career. Always consider consulting with a qualified tax attorney or your accountant when deciding on a legal structure. Remember that tax laws vary from state to state and are frequently changed and updated. Don't assume that what you know today about the law is going to apply tomorrow. Better safe than sorry by getting advice from someone whose job it is to know the laws as they pertain to you and your business.

Sole Proprietor

Becoming a sole proprietor is easy and the least costly of all business structures you can set up. If you don't form a corporation or partnership, you will automatically be considered a sole proprietor in the eyes of the Internal Revenue Service. Besides ease of set up, the advantages of being a sole proprietor are that all profits and business decisions are yours, as are the tax advantages your accountant can keep you abreast of. Financial management is relatively simple and can be performed with easy-to-learn computer software if desired.

Disadvantages include more potential difficulty obtaining financing when needed, and sole responsibility for all business decisions, actions, and liability. Any legal actions taken against debts or liability are the personal responsibility of a sole proprietor.

Partnerships

When two or more people engage in, and both contribute to, a business, they form a partnership. This may be advantageous in the home-based massage therapy business by easing the burdens of being self-employed. Two of these issues may include burnout from working alone or working too many hours without adequate time off.

A partnership should always include a written agreement, preferably legal, between the two partners. Advantages of such a business structure include decreasing business expenses, shared decision making and duties, possible increase in capital from the investment in the business from another person, and an increased likelihood of being able to get a business loan if needed.

Don't choose a business partner lightly. People aren't always going to agree on how a business should be run. Some won't make good decisions. Having a jointly owned business through a partnership is based on trust and sound judgment in who you choose to partner with. Because you can still be held personally responsible for liability issues and debt incurred without your consent, an LLC (limited liability corporation) may be the best way to protect your personal assets.

Corporations

A corporation is the most involved of all the business structures to set up. It is very important to have a tax attorney or knowledgeable accountant help you with this avenue should you choose to use it now or, at some point, in the future. Generally, if you hire several employees, own more than one location, or a franchise, a corporation may be the best option for your needs. Basically, a corporation is set up as a separate entity from you as the owner with a board of directors that oversees the policies and decision-making processes accordingly.

A major advantage to forming a corporation is to limit personal liability. As a sole proprietor, you can lose your personal assets if legal actions are taken against you for any reason.

The biggest disadvantage of forming a corporation is time and monetary expense to maintain or dissolve this type of in-depth legal structure.

A limited liability corporation, or LLC, is structured somewhere between a partnership and a corporation. LLCs may have similar benefits to a corporation, including tax shelters and protection from personal liability. These also have less complications than a traditional corporation.

There are specific laws that govern operating under a corporation and, again, you will need the assistance of a legal professional to advise you of the regulations within your locale.

In Office, On-Site, or Both?

As someone considering massage as a profession or for a new practitioner, you may be asking, what's right for me? Should I see clients only in my home-based office or studio? Should I travel to them? Or would it be best to try to combine the two?

Many massage therapists try to suit everyone's needs in the hopes that success and a larger income can be had. Although it may work out for a while, this is a big mistake that often leads to mental and physical exhaustion down the road. It is possible to do in-office and out-call massage, but good organization and planning are crucial to successfully managing both for extended periods of time.

In Office

Providing massage strictly from your home office is the convenient answer. First and foremost is the advantage of saving on travel and business overhead expenses. To work from home you simply walk from your home living space to your home working space. The money you save on travel, rent, and additional utility costs often translates into more money in your pocket. The in-office option also saves the time it would take to travel to on-site appointments and could possibly allow you to schedule an additional in-office appointment or two a day. Add the familiarity of routine and it seems the ideal choice.

However, one of the downsides of working solely from your home office is, ironically, also one of the advantages. Familiarity of routine often turns to boredom, which is heightened by the solitary environment massage therapists typically work in. This isolation can easily become a stress to some practitioners who may, in time, feel the desire for other adult interaction beyond the relative silence commonly employed in the massage setting.

Another consideration is the potential of your home office being located in a remote area, which creates a very real possibility of not generating enough business to make a living.

On-Site

On-site massage is also referred to as out-call massage. This is where you pack up your massage chair or table, linens, cleaning supplies, lotions, and music, and travel to your client's home, hotel, place of business, or wellness event. On-site work may be performed in airport waiting areas, at hospitals or doctor's offices, in shopping centers, and at festivals and fairs. This type of massage work is very inviting to those who enjoy being around larger groups of people.

Mobile massage's distinct advantage is it affords the opportunity of seeing new places and faces every day. The isolation issue many home practitioners face is far less likely for the massage therapist who travels.

Another attractive feature of out-call work is an increase in pay. Most practitioners do (and should) raise their hourly rate for on-site massage work. This rate increase may be a general increase or it may be in the form of charging extra for mileage. Some may charge for both. As an example: I may charge fifty dollars per client hour in my office, but if I drive to your home to provide a one-hour therapeutic massage session, you'll likely pay an additional twenty-five dollars or more depending on driving distance.

Because an on-site massage therapist working in public areas usually will provide services for a number of people in the course of the day, sessions are sometimes limited to ten, twenty, or thirty minutes. For these types of sessions, a commonly charged rate is one dollar per minute of massage service provided. If massage is for a group of people such as those employed in a doctor's office, a practitioner may offer a group rate instead of the standard dollar-per-minute charge.

Now the flip side of this coin is you are moving and setting up your equipment every day versus leaving your home office set up. Inclement weather may become the time when transporting equipment back and forth becomes the most cumbersome. The increase in risk of injury or strain from transferring equipment to and from vehicles and buildings day in and day out is another potential reality.

Then you must add the need to plan your daily schedule in a much more organized fashion due to travel times and possibly different massage locations. The need for additional safety precautions (remember you may be going to stranger's homes, hotel rooms, and other unfamiliar places) must also be taken into consideration as you make your decision on doing out-call massage.

Both?

What happens if you want to try both? Make organization the No. 1 priority. This means not only organizing your work schedule but also your home and family schedule down to the hour. It consists of coordinating appointments for home client sessions with those where you'll see clients at their home, hotel, business, or elsewhere. For safety, it's always prudent to make sure someone knows where you are and how long you'll be there. Some practitioners use an answering service. This is helpful with the security issue as well as for convenience in scheduling.

Combining in-office and on-site massage therapy can be done, but many practitioners will opt for one or the other as their primary work option. You may want to have one set of equipment for your home office and a separate set for travel, but be aware that having two sets of equipment and supplies incurs nearly double the expense of what you may have planned on initially. Ultimately, it will be worth it should you choose the route of doing both in-office and on-site or, out-call, massage.

Target Clientele

Again, as a new massage therapist or one who hasn't seen the amount of business income you might like to have, you may think you should accept everyone who calls or knocks on your door for massage. Initially, you will likely do just that in order to get your name out there. Yet it won't take long to see that working with an eighty-nine-year-old elderly client is going to take far different preparation and technique than what is required for a 220-pound male power lifter. Just like working in multiple locations, working on all types of people using lots of different massage techniques and modalities will afford you variety, but may also serve to overwhelm. When all is said and done, it may prove to be too exhausting to maintain. As in all things, finding balance that suits your particular needs is important.

Who Are You Drawn To?

Take notice of the people you enjoy, are drawn to, or like to work with. Do you have a natural interest in the elderly or children? Do you prefer to work with athletes, just men, or just women? Are you fascinated in the changes that take place during pregnancy and find yourself drawn to pre- and postnatal care?

If you've been a massage therapist for a while, you're new to the game, or you're just considering the profession, knowing the group of people you're naturally drawn to as your potential primary clientele is useful especially if you decide to specialize at some point in one of the many different massage therapy modalities.

What Type of Massage Do You Want to Do?
In conjunction with knowing who your target client might be, you might consider the types of massage you want to offer. This is not in reference to specialization that requires further training than what is typically only moderately addressed in standard massage training programs. This will be addressed later on in the book.

Is your primary goal to offer stress relief through relaxation massage? Are you interested in working with people who have muscle and joint pain, dysfunction, or injury? Do you want to provide comfort and basic human touch to the elderly who might not otherwise receive it due to living alone? Part of your hands-on training in massage school will be to work on fellow students, school or clinic volunteers, or friends and family. This presents an opportunity to pay attention to the many different types of people you could be working with as a licensed practitioner. It may be the perfect time to consider the types of massage you want to provide and those groups of people you may want to focus on working with later when your education is complete.

When starting out in the massage profession, it's a good idea to ask questions of yourself to assess where you can focus your interests and best utilize your particular talents and skills. Seasoned therapists should also consider doing this assessment from time to time to keep their practice from becoming lifeless and boring.

Massage Studio Design and Function
Perhaps one of the more fun aspects of setting up a home-based massage therapy business is planning out your massage studio or office. Here's where you begin to put the dream into the business part of the equation.

Where?
Assuming all the legal conditions, if there are any, have been met, it's time to plan your space. Ideally a separate room with its own entrance is the best plan for a home-based operation. With this type of setup, you needn't keep the rest of the house polished to a shine and it allows for a more professional atmosphere than when a client must walk through areas of your personal living space. It may be possible to have a separate room but not have a private entrance. If this is the case, it necessitates

keeping clutter to a minimum and putting pets in areas where they won't be greeting, licking, rubbing against, or possibly biting clients who are entering. Always keep safety first and foremost in your mind. No matter how much you love your pet and think they would never hurt someone, better safe than sorry. Besides, you may love animals yet your client may not. Allergies are also something to be aware of, so keeping pets separated as well as the home clean and tidy is essential.

If you don't have a separate room available, consider what other less-trafficked area of the home might make a suitable massage space. Consider a sunroom or a portion of the living room or family room. Never, and I repeat, never use a bedroom as a massage space. The reasons may or may not be obvious but I'll state them anyway. A bedroom is designed to be used mainly for sleeping and sexual activity. Because massage is typically performed with a client partially or completely nude, providing massage therapy in a bedroom can create an association between massage and sex in the mind of your client regardless of how professional you are. The bedroom is also considered very personal space and someone you never met who has come to you as a client may decide that receiving massage there is a very uncomfortable situation that they prefer not to experience again. Remember that you only get one shot at a first impression, and providing massage from your bedroom may make it a negative one in your client's mind.

How Much Room Is Needed?

Again, ideally you want an entire room dedicated to your massage studio or office. The room minimally would be approximately 10' x 10' or 10' x 12' to accommodate a table setup and some basic pieces of furniture for storage and client comfort. Smaller spaces can be used but this may restrict movement or create a claustrophobic atmosphere for some people. Of utmost importance, whether you have a separate room or must use space within your living quarters, is having enough room to move easily around all four sides of the massage table when you're working. If you do any type of stretching of the client's extremities or use table extension equipment, you must figure in additional space for this.

Are You Ready?

The first of the preliminaries of starting a home-based massage therapy business is asking yourself a variety of questions to determine where you, and your space, are ultimately at in terms of preparedness for this business venture. Only you can honestly assess if you have what it takes to begin a business and build it from the ground up.

Real-Life Story

Working from home can be a challenge if you have pets. I have a cat who knows that he is the king of the castle and heartily dislikes not having full roam of the house. One time when I was in session with a client (thankfully a very easy-going client), my cat escaped his confines and tiptoed around me and under my massage table. My client was lying in a prone position with her face in the face cradle as she talked to me and she suddenly squealed and then starting laughing. I stopped working and asked her what happened and she said, "Your cat just reached up and cuffed my nose!" Very fortunately he was only playing, and he has no front claws! From that point on he was no longer confined with only a pet gate, but placed in a closed bedroom.

Following your assessment, be sure to check your state, county, and local laws governing permits and zoning. You may not even be able to have a home-based business where you are. Knowing that up front will be less disheartening than doing all the other tasks of setting up shop then having to change course. The bottom line is making sure you meet any and all requirements and regulations; this will save you time and hassle, and ease the start-up process.

Determining your business structure may seem daunting, but again, it's one of the beginning steps to forming your business. Most massage therapists begin as self-employed sole proprietors of their practice, and a good portion of those practicing massage will never deviate from the sole-proprietorship structure. However, it helps to at least know what is required for each division in the case that your business builds beyond your initial expectations or you decide to take a different route than originally planned. Remembering to consult with a qualified tax attorney or accountant as your business needs change will make planning for change much more simple.

Another important concept that needs to be stressed is not being the all-purpose therapist. Many new or seasoned practitioners form, or buy into, the belief that massage therapy is a luxury that only those who are able can afford, which makes them question if they can make a viable living being a massage provider. Thus, they all too frequently make common mistakes that have them trying to be the therapist to meet all needs. This type of therapist frequently works both from his home office and his client's home or workplace. He frequently changes his weekly work hours to accommodate everyone else's schedules. Afraid of not getting enough business or making enough money, he sees every type of client from young children to the muscle-bound power lifter. He makes every attempt to be the ultimate therapist to each and every client he sees.

Here's your reality check: The ultimate massage therapist does not exist. Just as your clients are human, so are you. Attempting to be it all and do it all is a recipe for disaster, both personally and professionally. Determine what type of business structure and size you want to start with, where you want to conduct business (your home office exclusively, on-site, or both), and who your primary target clientele might be. When you make your initial determinations in these areas, you can move on to the task of setting up your place of business.

It's All in the Planning

The business plan is instrumental in the success of your massage therapy practice. It's like a road map that shows you where you're going and how to get there. A plan will help you define what you want for your business, and by putting it in writing, you'll gain clarity and insight. It may simply be used for your own purposes to determine your main objectives, explain why you're doing what you do, what your goals are—both short- and long-term—and your plan of action to reach them. This road map is useful to the seasoned practitioner who may need or want to revive a tired practice by re-evaluating why she remains in the massage profession or what new goals she may wish to set for herself.

An effective business plan is also helpful for obtaining financing when necessary. If you need to secure financing, depending on the size of the loan, the bank will very likely want to see a professional, detailed business plan before they talk money with you.

A basic business plan should begin with a summary page of what your business is about. Some readers may never read past this page, so it's important to make every word count. It should consist of a precise description of what type of business you have (massage therapy), the people you serve, and how specifically you will help them with your services and products. It further addresses what goals you intend to reach with your business and how you will market your practice to see them to fruition. The emphasis, especially for financing purposes, will be on the marketing component. Specifics are needed for what you intend to do strategically to market your business, a timeline for completion, and what it will cost to accomplish what you set out to do. Define as precisely as you can how marketing techniques will allow your business to be profitable.

Following the summary page is the body of the plan. The body will give a more thorough description of the business. This includes specific services and products, local competition, pricing, marketing plans, financial data showing a business budget, profit and loss statements (if an existing business), cash flow (if an existing business), and any supporting documents such as tax returns, lease agreements for business equipment (if applicable), copies of licenses, and bank or credit union financial statements.

As you can see, creating a business plan can be daunting or at least seem that way. The best approach is to thoroughly think through your business ideas, hopes, goals, and requirements, and write them down in a rough draft. Then use the sample business plan outline provided on page 23 as a template to follow as you fill in the details. In addition, visit the Small Business Administration website, www.sba.gov, for more information on forming the business plan that best suits your own needs.

It's important to note that every business is unique and will use different aspects of a business plan. Most business owners will research several plan templates to determine which aspects they require and which ones they don't. For the most part if a plan is for personal use, it typically needn't be as in-depth as one that will be used to secure a loan.

Write a Mission Statement

A mission statement clearly and concisely defines your business and what its objectives are. This is a typical adjunct to a business plan presented to a lending institution when you need a loan. This statement is also helpful for reminding yourself and when describing what you do to other people. Some business owners will write a mission statement of three or four paragraphs but I don't think that's always necessary. In my opinion, a mission statement can be highly effective even though it's only a few sentences in length. Thinking of, and writing, a mission statement should not be taken lightly even if it's only a single sentence long.

A standard massage therapy mission statement might look like this:

> Our mission is to provide relaxation, facilitation of self-healing, and improved well-being through therapeutic massage. Our practitioners are highly trained, caring individuals skilled in several types of manual therapies developed to address a client's needs in a professional comfortable setting. We strive to provide the most beneficial massage experience and ongoing education for the community we serve.

Cover Page:
Includes the title of the business, owner's name, address, and contact information.

Table of Contents:
A table of contents will provide the reader, at a glance, all the components of the business plan and where to find them.

Executive Summary:
This section consists of the business plan highlights. Again, because this could well be the only page that gets read, it's important to really make a great impression on the reader. Even though the summary is at the beginning of the plan, it's most beneficial to write this piece after the entire plan is completed and keep it clear, concise, and relatively short. Include:

- Business mission statement

- What type of service and products you will provide (what do you do?)

- Whom you will serve (who is your demographic market?)

- How you will market your business (how will you sell your services?)

- What sets you apart from similar businesses (what do you offer that others may not?)

- Your loan needs (if any)

- Future plans for the business (considering expansion, selling products, or other?)

Body:
This part contains three sub-sections consisting of business operations, financial analysis, and supporting documents. For each include the following:

Business Operations

- Business structure (sole proprietor?)

- Strengths and assets (what are your qualifications to run a business?)

- Training and abilities (what license[s] or certification[s] do you hold?)

- Permits, business license, insurance—health, liability, disability, homeowners—coverage (do you have some or all of these in place?)

- Demographic market (who will use your services and how will you stand out from other similar businesses?)

- Marketing plan (how will you promote and advertise your services to get business?)

- Record keeping (who will do your accounting and handle financial aspects of your business? If it's you, how will you do this? Manually? By computer? Explain.)

Financial Analysis

- A projected initial annual income (based on an average of what area massage therapists are earning, the number of client hours you plan to work, and the rates you've set for your services)

- Rates you'll charge for your services, which include introductory specials, group discounts, sliding scale fees, and other discount options

- The number of clients you have determined you need to have in order to reach your income goals

- Start-up worksheets for equipment and supplies needed, monthly operational costs, and a business expense budget

- Loan requirements: how much, when it's needed, and why

Supporting Documents

- The past three years tax returns (for existing businesses)

- Copies of bank statements

- Copies of licenses/certifications held (including business license and any permits)
- Copies of resumes of business owner (or employees if applicable)
- Recent credit report (not usually necessary as lending institutions can access easily)
- Any pertinent information that may help secure a loan (i.e., news articles on your business, charitable causes supported through your business, personal or business references)

Here are some examples of good and poor single-sentence mission statements. These simple statements can help you to begin to clearly consider what your business's mission is:

- **Good:** Our mission is to help athletes *get back to their sport sooner* after injury and strain by providing therapeutic massage and education to possibly prevent future injury.
- **Poor:** Our mission is to help athletes by providing manual therapies for injury and strain.
- **Good:** Our mission is to provide *pain relief* to chronic pain sufferers in a safe, comfortable environment using professional massage therapy tailored to clients' specific needs.
- **Poor:** Our mission is to provide holistic health care to those in need.
- **Good:** Our mission is to *ease pain and discomforts* that come with advancing age through massage and soothing touch.
- **Poor:** Our mission is to help elderly people to feel better with massage.

Although the second point in each example is also accurate, it is not as specific a description of what the massage practitioner actually does to help a client. First and foremost, your client wants to know what your services will do for them and they want it defined in a short, specific, and understandable format. The italicized portions are what your client is going to hear above all else.

As a practitioner, you may not simply work with athletes, those in chronic pain, or the elderly. You may work with a blend of different clients presenting an array of reasons for being in your massage office. The above examples are purposely oversimplified to clarify the concept. The important thing is to clearly state it for yourself no matter how long the statement is, then keep zeroing in until you make it as concise as possible in relation to the vision you have for your business. Remember that the more simplified your mission statement is, the easier it is to explain.

State Your Vision

Now that you can clearly explain what your mission is, what is the bigger vision behind what you do? If the mission statement is what and how, the vision statement is why. A vision statement states the general purpose for the work you do. Some people omit the vision statement and go with just the mission statement. Others may opt to combine the two. The choice is yours but it may be effective to create two individual statements initially to really get clear on what, how, and why you do what you do.

The following are some examples of good and poor single-sentence vision statements. They are a good starting point to get you thinking about what your business vision may look like. As you might notice, it's a very easy process to combine your mission statement with your vision statement.

- **Good:** To help athletes return to their chosen sports more quickly
- **Poor:** To ease strained muscles through manual therapies
- **Good:** To assist chronic pain sufferers with the ability to take on the tasks of daily living
- **Poor:** People in pain experience massage with positive results
- **Good:** To allow elderly people to receive the comfort of human touch in addition to improving age-related pain and immobility
- **Poor:** Integrating the mind, body, and spirit through massage

The good statements address a purpose. The poor ones, though accurate, are too vague. Remember to hone in on both your mission and vision statements. It may help to create a values list to help you further define them. Typical values may include:

- Respectful communication

- Commitment to the education of the community about benefits of massage therapy
- Demonstration of compassion, empathy, and caring to the specific needs of all clients
- Strong ethics, boundaries, and integrity

A combined mission and vision statement based on your business's values might look like this:

Our mission is to provide relaxation, facilitation of self-healing, and improved well-being through therapeutic massage. Our practitioners are highly trained, caring individuals skilled in several types of manual therapies developed to address a client's needs in a professional, comfortable setting. We strive to provide the most beneficial massage experience and ongoing education for the community we serve.

We feel strongly that our clients' well-being come first and we take pride in our efforts to portray this foundational premise of our practice. Through respect, compassion, and a dedication to the craft, our practitioners present a unified effort to helping clients return to more vibrant health through education, the use of scientific therapeutic massage techniques, and unequaled commitment to a higher quality of living.

Real-Life Story

A very special, elderly blind woman was referred to me by her daughter. The daughter's mother had just had a very serious illness and needed comfort care as the family was not quite sure she was going to live much longer. She and I met once a week in my office to provide very gentle massage for her and, surprisingly to her and her family, she is still seeing me to this day nearly five years later. She believes firmly she would not be here, at almost ninety years old, if it wasn't for her regular massage. And each week, she thanks me and tells me she loves me. It doesn't get any better than that.

Determine Your Goals

Now that you've got your mission, vision, and values firmly detailed, make a list of what you want to achieve with your business through goal setting. Your goals timeline can include what you are looking to achieve in a month's time, a year's time, and even a projected outlook for five or more years down the road. In fact, if you are writing a business plan for financial purposes, you will want to make long-range goals so that the lending institution can determine how much of a risk it might be doing business with you.

Prioritize the goals that are most relevant, and important, to you. For example, these may include getting ten new clients per month through marketing and promotional efforts, doing three wellness events per year, or earning $75,000 within five years.

Beyond any potential for a relationship with a bank or other lender, it's just good sense to set short- and long-term goals for your business to ensure its success.

If the business plan is for your own use, try to also include personal goals that tie in to your business. Personal goals can inspire and give you a strong feeling of working toward something. Examples here may include earning enough profit in the first year of business to take your family on a one-week vacation, scheduling regular monthly massage for yourself for self care, or planning to have one evening a week as a take-out dinner night to help with time management.

Again, limit personal goals to a plan for your own use. For financial-lending purposes, stick to facts and business-related goals that help the bank determine whether or not to lend you the money you're asking for.

Goal setting for business or personal use can be incredible fun. It's using your imagination, determination, and your skills to create your business and personal life. Beyond just thinking of what you'd like to achieve, putting your aspirations on paper breathes life into them because writing them down, or otherwise capturing them in a tangible manner, takes them one step further from dream to reality.

The goals you set for yourself should be clearly stated, written in present tense (not the future or you may never reach them), and they should be realistic to achieve. Never use words like *want, try, should, not,* and *if* in your goal statements. Whenever possible have a deadline for accomplishment so the goal doesn't stay open-ended indefinitely.

Keep your goals in front of you at all times. Review them daily and realize that some may need adjusting from time to time. Remember that goals still mean nothing if action to bring them to fruition isn't taken.

Many people use the SMART acronym to remember what they want to do within their goal-setting endeavors. Though different business or life coaches and advisers have altered meanings for the term, for our purposes we'll use the basic interpretation, which stands for specific, measurable, achievable, realistic, and timeline.

- **Specific:** Choose a goal that is specifically worded. "I choose to make more money" is a common goal people set for themselves. Though it is stated in present tense, which is a better option than the "I want" futuristic statement, it is also so vague that you wouldn't know when you've reached your goal. A better goal statement would be "I choose to earn an additional $500 per month." Choose your target wisely.
- **Measurable:** Along with specificity, it's important to be able to measure your goals in order to recognize when you've hit your target. Instead of stopping at "I choose to earn an additional $500 per month," clarify further with "I choose to earn an additional $500 per month by selling ten massage gift certificates."
- **Achievable:** Is your goal achievable for you? Stating a goal that is beyond reach only sets you up for failure and the probability that you won't set, or strive for, further goals in the future.
- **Reasonable:** Again, ask if this goal is something you can reasonably expect to achieve. If not, re-word your goal until it's something you know you may need to stretch to reach, but that is definitely attainable.
- **Timeline:** Within your goal, set a time frame for completion. Leaving goals open-ended is a recipe for incompletion and ends up filed in the "someday" category.

Written Goal Statements

The written form of goal setting is perhaps easiest because it's least time consuming and most basic. Putting goals on paper is a simple matter of listing exactly what you want to achieve using the SMART technique mentioned above.

For the written method, some people keep a journal or goal diary that is convenient to review and carry with them. Goals can also be written on specialty paper that catches the eye or has a background design with particular significance, in a simple spiral-bound notebook, or even on sticky notes where they can be strategically placed within the home and work area and seen easily. Writing goals on paper adds tangibility to your dreams and aspirations. See the "Goal Setting Worksheet" on page 30 to get you started thinking and writing down your goals.

Goal Title: _____

_____

Completion Date:

_____

Specific Goal to Achieve:

_____

_____

_____

_____

_____

Why Do I Want This?

_____

_____

_____

_____

Action Plan Steps:

1._____

2._____

3._____

4._____

5._____

Vision Boards or Collages

Because many people are visually oriented, a vision board or collage might have more appeal with your goal-setting project. A simple collage on heavy poster-stock paper or thicker foam board can be designed in an hour or two. With a collage all that is required is to collect photos or images—your own or torn from old magazines—that best represent what you want to achieve. You can also use a computer-graphics program to design images and use text to give meaning and depth to your goal-setting poster. Once you've collected the images and text that best define your goals, affix them to your poster board and put up the collage in a prominent place where you can see it frequently.

Vision boards are the same premise as a collage, yet often a vision board is made for each goal-setting area. I have a separate vision board for financial and career goals, home and family goals, health goals, and dream goals. By keeping them separate, I can focus on any one vision board with goals that require more attention to achieve than another. Create a vision board in the same way as a collage, but don't feel you have to fill the entire space with images and text. For some people a cluttered vision board may signify chaos versus specific goals to reach for. Before making either the simple collage or the more in-depth vision boards, carve time out of your day to really focus on what you want your boards to project to you when you look at them. If any image or text doesn't feel right to you, change it until it does. After all, you will be looking at this every day and you want it to feel good when you do.

Video Recordings

Video (or audio) recordings may have more appeal to those who prefer the spoken word to the written or visual goal-setting techniques. Video or audio requires some sort of device that can record a set amount of audio/video for you to clearly and concisely state the goals you set for yourself. A video recorder, digital camera with video, or some cell phones have these functions. Remember that because goals should be reviewed daily, video or audio recordings may not be as easy as picking up a notebook or viewing a vision board posted on your wall. Consider putting the audio on CD and listening to it in the car while driving or put it on an MP3 player or smartphone to listen to while walking or exercising. Transferring video to your computer makes your goals more readily accessible as well.

A computerized vision board is becoming a very popular way to record your goals in a multimedia production. This may be an optimal way to have your goals at your fingertips because they are created on your computer and easily accessible. Many are designed to play in the background as you work on the computer with the intent of positively instilling your goals into your subconscious mind. Specific vision board software is available or, with some multimedia programs, you can design your own. Designing your own digital vision board from scratch is a bit more advanced and it may be easier for some to simply acquire the software that includes image selections, audio selections, and even text affirmations and goals. These programs have the ability to fully customize your vision board to suit your personality and the specific goals you set for yourself.

Develop a Plan of Action

You have your goals determined and have included them in your business plan. You placed a copy on the bulletin board over your desk, on your computer as desktop wallpaper, and even have a sticky note stuck to your bathroom mirror. You visualize your goals daily and are excited and inspired in hopes of seeing each one to realization.

Now it's time to make a plan of action. This is where the phrase "plan your work and work your plan" comes from. Written goals, no matter how much fun and how inspiring, mean nothing if you don't take the actions necessary to see them take form.

If you hope to achieve your goal to get ten new clients in the next month, you may need to contact fifty people. How will you do that? Can you contact each of your existing clients and simply ask them to refer a friend? Would it be beneficial to work out a joint venture with an area business owner to cross promote one another?

If you want to participate in a wellness event to promote your business, who do you need to contact? How will your participation take form, and can you supply educational and promotional materials to those you work with at the event?

And if $75,000 is your five-year goal, what will you need to earn yearly, monthly, and weekly to reach that goal? Can you break the figures down and determine how many clients you need to see or what else you can provide in the form of gift certificate or product sales to reach that goal? What else could you do to add to your plan to reach that five-year goal? Can you teach a partner-massage or stress-reduction class?

Short-term goals are generally smaller in scope and therefore easier to make happen. Short-term goals should always be made with foresight in regards to how they relate to the longer range goals. In other words, short-term goal setting should always be considered steps toward reaching long-range, or bigger, goals. Don't skip over smaller goals to get to the bigger ones thinking small means trivial. Sometimes we set our sights on the bigger picture and forget it takes smaller steps to get there.

The way to avoid being overwhelmed in achieving your goals is to chunk down the big goals into smaller goals. Then break down smaller goals further into manageable action steps you can take to see them to completion in the time span you've allotted. As you complete short-term goals, ask yourself if they have moved you closer to your longer-range goals. It's great if they do, but if they don't, rethink the next set of short-term goals you make. If you hadn't guessed, you will forever be making goals. Not setting any more after you achieve your initial goals will only serve to create stagnation in your business and bore you to tears. Keep your business, and your life, exciting by setting newer and loftier goals.

As you reach each goal, no matter the size, make sure to acknowledge your achievements. Only you can give yourself the true motivation and confidence to move on to bigger and better accomplishments.

How Will You Build Your Dream?

Start your road to business success with a solid written plan. Include what your business is all about, why you're providing this service, who you're projecting to provide to, and how you'll make that happen. List the goals you want to set for your business, both short and long term. If your business plan is for financing purposes, be sure to be clear, concise, and highly detailed with a timeline for completion of those goals. A clear business plan shows a lender that you take your business seriously and have a viable plan to succeed. It will give you credibility and make a financial institution more likely to consider you a worthwhile risk.

Add your personal goals to the plan if it is for your own individual use, but leave them off if the plan is to be presented to a lender. Even if you don't write an actual business plan (which is not recommended), set goals for your business and your personal use. Compare both lists and see if they are compatible with one another. If not, rethink them until they are. Use one of the techniques described to detail what you aspire toward and use the SMART protocol that will help you bring greater clarity to what you want and the steps to achieve it.

Always keep your goals something to stretch for without making them so out of reach that you give up on attaining them, and be sure smaller goals are stepping-stones to reaching the longer-range goals you've set for yourself. If they're not, change your goals. It's not rocket science. Do what works, change what doesn't, and ultimately make sure each step is directed toward the bigger picture. Lastly, reward yourself upon reaching any goal, large or small, and then set new ones. With each goal you set, take action steps and achieve it. You will find your confidence growing by leaps and bounds even as your feeling of being overwhelmed lessens dramatically.

04 Outfitting the Massage Studio

The title of this chapter is "Outfitting the Massage Studio." Here, the word *studio* could just as easily be replaced with *office*. Consider each of these words and decide which resonates more with your personality and the style of massage you do or would like to do. *Studio* often connotes an artistic ambience, where the word *office* may sound more professional and businesslike. Because massage therapy is frequently referred to as a healing art, *studio* may be entirely appropriate. However, massage is also steadily making its way into the mainstream medical world, so the word *office* may be the better choice because it has a more professional presentation than the word *studio*. This is a minor detail perhaps, but certainly one to consider depending on your personality type, your massage style, and the business image you wish to project.

When you set up your office or studio there are many aspects to consider. The first determination should be whether you desire a more clinical atmosphere or a spa-like environment. A massage space should always portray a certain ambience to soothe and calm. Though a clinic is soothing, it also typically has a very simple look and feel. This setting may have a few nature prints on the walls but overall the look is crisp and clean. There may also be a need for a larger working space or greater accessibility if you will be seeing individuals with certain medical conditions or mobility issues.

A spa-type setting may have a bit more character to define its relaxing attributes and contain items like candles, fountains, mirrors, nature items, and other amenities specially suited for client comfort.

A common mistake is to clutter the area with too much decor or color, making the space's appearance more chaotic than serene. Neutral color palettes may be best suited to the massage environment, with a slightly bolder color for accent. Too many colors or too much decor can overstimulate the senses, leaving a client feeling distressed and unable to fully relax regardless of how wonderful your massage is.

Another consideration is the type of flooring in your massage space. Though carpet is easy for the therapist to stand on—comfortable and generally soft to bare feet—it is also more difficult to keep clean and may present an allergenic environment unsuitable for some clients. Area rugs may serve as an alternative for client comfort but these must have a non-slip back to prevent them from sliding. Keep in mind that area rugs may present a hazard to some people with mobility issues. Other types of flooring that may be suitable are hardwood, vinyl, or synthetic-wood fabricated materials. These generally have either built-in cushioning or some sort of padding installed beneath, which makes them easier on the massage therapist's legs and feet. Cleaning these types of flooring is far easier than carpeting and usually has a reduced incidence of allergic reaction. In a home office the flooring is usually already in place, so work with what you have if finances don't allow for change.

Beyond comfort, the most important feature of a massage space is privacy. Even a dedicated room used for massage purposes needs to have a "no general access policy" that keeps family and pets from frequent coming and going. With this policy in place, your space remains the soothing respite you want it to be for your clientele whether you are in session or not.

Real-Life Story

Because I have a creative side, I was able to totally immerse myself in the delight of designing and reconstructing my home massage office. Yet because my massage room was located toward the back of my house, it took some effort to separate home and workspace since clients had to walk through my sunroom and hallway to access it. To remedy the situation, I simply closed off the entrance to the rest of the house with the use of accordion-style doors I could open at the end of the day. Not only was this simple door structure effective in partitioning the massage space from the rest of my home, it also served to keep pets contained. In addition, I had a very simple, small half-bathroom built into the massage room so clients would not need to use the main bathroom of my home.

Essential Massage Equipment

Regardless if your business is a studio or an office, it will require much of the same equipment. With specialization other supplies and equipment become necessary, but everyone starts out needing the same essentials to operate their home-based massage therapy business.

An important consideration to factor in is available space. If your space is less than the minimum mentioned previously, then you will likely choose only the bare necessities. Yet if space allows and storage is available, you may have the options of using a larger massage table or being able to offer multiple bodywork modalities that may require more equipment.

Massage Table

Massage tables can be portable or stationary. Though both are made for maximum functionality, the portable table is designed specifically for its ability to be moved within the room, stored, or transported. Stationary tables are quite durable for heavy usage and frequently have underneath storage areas. This storage space can make them a great option for those with a small massage space. On average, if you will need to move the table more than a few times per year, choose a lighter-weight portable table that folds for storage or transport. If you have a dedicated space for an electric-operated stationary table, you may find this option to be optimal (though considerably more expensive) because of its versatility with changing position and height. Most therapists will want a minimum of three feet of working space around the table to allow for stretching the client and proper ergonomic positioning for you to work most effectively and avoid potential injury or strain. Depending on the room or space size, you may not be afforded the minimum around the table perimeter. If not, consider angling the massage table so the ends are facing into a corner. As you plan for the dimensions of your massage table in accordance with your space, keep in mind any extension accessories you may want to include such as the face cradle and armrest that lengthen the table or the side-arm extensions that increase the width of the table.

Massage Table Coverings

This covers a broad range of items under the term *linens*. Sheets, blankets, pillows, and face-cradle covers are all basic necessities. All but face-cradle covers can be found in retail stores that carry housewares. Alternatively, all of these items can be purchased through massage-supply companies. Sheets and blankets sold specifically for massage use are sized to smoothly fit the narrower span of a massage table. Twin-size fitted sheets purchased locally are slightly wider than a massage table but are still a usable option. Some massage therapists opt for disposable sheets and face-cradle covers for ease of use, sanitation, and less laundry to do. These may be more appropriate for on-site massage than for daily use in the home office and have a higher environmental impact than cloth sheets, which are washable. Disposable face-cradle covers are useful for chair massage or for use at massage events where a large number of clients would make doing laundry impossible.

Massage Chair

I've listed massage chairs under essentials for those practitioners who will want to do on-site massage at least occasionally. Massage chairs, like tables, come in a variety of styles and prices. One style is called a desktop model. This is a smaller unit designed to hook to a desktop or other flat surface and has an adjustable chest cushion and face cradle for the client to lean into. This model is handy as a lightweight portable unit for on-site work in schools, doctor's offices, or other areas where desks are plentiful or where space may be limited. Other massage-chair models are full size, and though still portable, may be bulky and only slightly lighter than a massage table. Like massage tables, massage chairs can be purchased at massage-supply companies or through many international and auction sites across the Internet with variable costs and quality.

Towels

A variety of different-size towels is important to keep in the massage area. These are also easily acquired in larger stores that carry home products. Debatable is whether to buy inexpensive and lower-quality towels or purchase more expensive, yet higher-quality ones. Inexpensive towels are easy to wash and dry, and if they become stained they can be used as cleaning cloths. Better-quality towels, on the other hand, can more readily tolerate frequent washings, which may make them worth the higher cost. Also consider purchasing matching or coordinating towels. As with the design and decor of the massage space, too many colors and patterns can add to a chaotic look in the storage area. Regardless of the towels you buy, when it's time to buy new, consider donating old ones to animal shelters in order to reuse and recycle.

Storage Cabinet or Shelf

Even something such as a small bookcase will suffice to hold linens, towels, and lubricants. Save money by picking up one at a resale shop or yard sale, and repaint it to match the massage-space decor. One with doors can give a cleaner look to the space by hiding the linens, towels, or other supplies. If these items are on an open shelf, either roll the towels or place like items in small, attractive baskets. If nothing else, at least be sure all items are folded and placed or stacked neatly on the shelves.

Lubricants

Lubricants are the massage oils, creams and butters, lotions, gels, and powders you will use on clients. These can be purchased through massage-supply companies, or in natural-living or health-food stores. Some massage products or can be handcrafted from a combination of natural plant-based carrier oils and essential oils. Buy lubricants in smaller supplies when just starting out because some become rancid over a relatively short period of time. Keep in mind that some clients will have allergies or aversions to smells so keep an unscented product on hand.

All lubricants have a shelf life. This is the period of time before it expires and must be discarded. Standard massage oils have a shelf life of about one year if stored away from direct sunlight. Lotions, creams, butters, and gels have a life of approximately two years. Powder-based products may last even longer if stored away from moisture. Most manufacturer brands of lubricants contain preservatives such as parabens, to which some people are allergic. Major brands will also carry organic lines that don't contain parabens but will likely have shorter storage time.

Other lubricants are natural plant-based oils that can be purchased locally in natural-living or health-food stores. Some of these oils are sweet almond, jojoba, grape seed, and avocado. Natural oils, when in their pure form (pure plant or seed extracts without added ingredients), will not have the same shelf life as massage manufacturers' products so should be purchased in small quantities to avoid spoilage.

Types of Massage Lubricants

Oils: These are made from plant, nut, or seed extractions. They provide a protective, moisturizing barrier for the skin and have the highest glide factor. This glide factor is what determines how well the practitioner's hands slide over the client's skin during massage treatment. It is very useful when performing long strokes over the body such as those done in Esalen massage. Practitioners must be aware that certain clients may have allergies to nut oils.

Lotions: Made with a combination of oil, water, and thickening agents, lotions are a penetrating, moisturizing product with slightly less glide factor than oil. Lotions are often preferred by clients who don't like the greasy feeling of their skin after massage or the possibility of staining clothing. Lotions are effective for use in techniques like deep-tissue massage that employ more precise and controlled movement of a practitioner's hands.

Creams and body butter: These products have a creamier consistency, yet higher fat content than lotions. They are versatile in that more can be used to produce the glide factor, and less used for more controlled massage techniques. Body butters solidify at colder temperatures and liquefy at warmer temps.

Gels: Gels are oil that have been thickened and usually contain some sort of wax that easily melts to allow glide over warm skin. These products are similar in versatility to creams and body butters.

Powders: Typically powders are cornstarch based. Not as frequently used as the other types of lubricants, powders biggest advantages are not leaving a greasy feel on the skin or pulling body hair.

Office Equipment and Supplies

As with any business you start up, you must purchase or lease office supplies to get you up and running. From paper products to the equipment that will make your practice run more smoothly, this is potentially one of the more costly investments in your home-based massage therapy business. Stick with the essentials at first and add more as your business grows. Also keep in mind the space you will have to accommodate office equipment and supplies. Will you have a separate office, a corner of the massage room, or simply a desk in your living room? Judge the amount of equipment you obtain by your needs, which includes the space it will take to house them. Keeping your office supplies in one location will help exponentially to maintain order for your client records, files, and other important documents.

Computer

Most homes already have at least one desktop or laptop computer. If that's the case, all the better. The computer can be a costly addition when first starting out in business. Whether you have to buy one or already have one, it will be helpful to have a graphics program in case you want to design your own business cards and literature, a good word-processing program, financial software for computerized bookkeeping, and Internet access. As the business advances, you may want to consider massage therapy–specific software for financial and client record keeping, client scheduling, and target clientele tracking. For those who will predominantly use digital means of record keeping, always back up your files somewhere other than your computer's hard drive. This is easily accomplished with any number of free online storage options. Another alternative is to keep records on removable memory sticks, cards, or flash drives. Backing up digital files is an easy aspect to overlook, but all it takes is one computer crash to lose client files, accounting records, and other documents that are difficult or impossible to recreate.

Telephone

Highly debated is whether to have a dedicated line for massage-office use only. The advantage of having a dedicated line is the professionalism it shows. The disadvantage is it's another monthly bill. Depending on where you live and operate your business, you may pay a higher monthly rate for a separate business line. Many therapists will save costs by using their standard home phone and get a phone with a voice-mail system that has two or more in-boxes. This way, you can leave a message on the machine directing the caller to the in-box for massage therapy. For incoming calls during working hours, always answer the phone in a professional manner or let it go to voice mail. If you choose voice mail, always return calls promptly. Another option is a cell phone. As with a landline phone, it's important to leave a professional-sounding voice mail message for callers and to accept calls in a professional voice. By not making your family's home line accessible, a separate business phone line is also a useful safety precaution. A dedicated line also makes it easier to track your business-phone expenses for tax purposes.

Printer/Scanner/Copier/Fax

Again, most homes will have a printer of some sort along with a computer. A printer for your business is invaluable for client newsletters, business cards, and other literature. Remember, the more detailed graphics you use for your literature needs, the higher the quality printer you will need. Keep the cost of ink cartridges in mind when choosing a printer. Often what seems to be a great deal in a printer ends up being much less cost effective when figuring the price of the ink. The range of prices and types of printers varies as much as the ink cartridges it takes to print with, so it pays to shop around. Many styles of printers are multifunctional. Models often include fax, copy, and scan capabilities. The multifunction printer is a helpful space saver for those therapists with limited room for individual pieces of equipment. As convenient as it is to have a printer to print literature, it is equally beneficial at times to have fax, scan, and copy capabilities. The fax feature allows you to send copies of client SOAP notes to doctor's offices or insurance companies, for instance. (SOAP notes are the notes a massage therapist takes after a session with a client detailing the client's condition, plan of action, and results of treatment. See page 86 for more information.) Electronic fax (e-fax) is an alternative to having an actual fax machine that requires a telephone landline. For a monthly fee, faxes can be sent electronically through e-mail. Many smartphones and PDAs can receive a fax as well, making it convenient for massage therapists who travel for their work. Scanning is also a useful option when choosing a multifunction printer. With a scanner, a therapist can scan and copy important receipts, files, and other documents. These can then be forwarded to accountants, physicians' offices, clients, or other pertinent recipients. Alternatively, scanning documents is another means of creating a backup of physical paperwork in the event it is lost or destroyed.

Desk and Chair

Whether purchased new or bought at a thrift shop or at a yard sale, you will need a desk and chair to work at the computer and store office supplies and equipment. Try to find a chair that is as ergonomically correct as possible so that if you find yourself sitting for long periods, your neck, back, and legs will be comfortable and properly supported.

Paper Products

These will include standard 8½" x 11" stock for stationery, and business card and brochure stock if you choose to make your own business cards and literature. These items are readily available in larger retail stores and may be much less expensive than when purchased at office supply companies or online.

Filing Cabinets

Though some massage therapists will do much of their filing digitally, it cannot be stressed enough to have a backup plan. For most practitioners a simple filing cabinet with file folders is a great way to stay organized and keep all written or printed documents in one central location. With client files, accounting records, and receipts properly filed and labeled, locating the information you need becomes quick and easy. Because paper files can accumulate rapidly, it's vital to have an efficient and organized filing system in place.

Include sections for the following:

- Individual client files
- Monthly expense records and receipts
- Monthly income records, loan documents (if applicable)
- Permits and licenses (that don't have to be publicly displayed at the business location)

Client records will require the most organizing because they consist of the initial-intake forms, update information forms, and massage session SOAP notes. Creating subfiles for each client within the main file is optimal for maximum efficiency,

Cleaning and Sanitation

Most businesses require a high level of cleanliness and this is an obvious point. However, when you have a health-and-wellness business, you must remain diligent about maintaining a higher-than-normal level of sanitation. There may be some locales that will have regulations requiring regular yearly inspections of your massage location. Remember also that there may be times you will see clients with chronic conditions or terminal illnesses requiring an extra measure of precautionary sanitation. Great care must be taken in these situations so as not to compromise their already weakened immune system or your own health.

Laundry Detergent

Many lubricating oils and lotions will stain linens. In time, these linens will be unsightly and the oils on them will turn rancid and smell. Generally at this time they will need to be replaced with new ones. There are also many products that contain degreasers specially made for massage therapists that extend the life of linens. These can be purchased at most massage-supply stores or websites.

Disinfectant Cleaners

These can be standard all-purpose cleaning products or those that are organic in nature. Many massage therapists will prefer the organic products because they are less likely to irritate or be as strongly scented as the harsher store-bought cleaners on the market. Use proper judgment in choosing organic products to make sure they have disinfectant agents and are not just basic soap-based cleaning products.

Miscellaneous Supplies

Beyond the essentials, there are a number of different types of equipment and supplies that serve to increase the benefits and scope of the massage session you offer a client. The wide variety of options can also help make the massage you provide more relaxing and inviting.

The following list is considered miscellaneous, though some are highly useful for both you and your client. Many are inexpensive and readily accessible, so you might want to add them to your equipment sooner rather than later. Massage supplies change and suppliers add new items to their product lines all the time, so you may also wish to sign up to receive catalogs from supply companies to stay abreast of current trends in the field.

Hand-Held Massage Tools

These include simple pressure-point instruments, percussion, or vibratory tools, and electric- or battery-operated massagers. Though most clients are going to prefer a

Health and Safety Inspections

Many health inspections are impromptu. The reason for this is inspectors don't want you to pass inspection ONLY because you know one is coming. Impromptu inspections will show how you follow health and safety practices on an everyday basis.

In Tennessee, health inspections consist of making sure the following are adhered to:

■ Working fire extinguishers and adequate number of functioning smoke detectors per square footage on the premises

■ A clean waiting area with a minimum of one chair

■ A current copy of massage therapist's license available for inspection

■ Garbage and clutter removal

■ Equipment, massage table, and bathroom facilities clean and sanitized

■ Overall cleanliness of space

■ Linens, towels, and other client coverings cleaned and sanitized between uses

■ Restroom available and equipped with toiletries, hot and cold running water, hand-washing facilities

■ Explanation of draping techniques and a drape provided for each client. (Drapes are some sort of covering for the client's privacy and comfort. This is usually a sheet, towel, or spa wrap.)

Each section of the inspection is assigned point value. The massage establishment must meet a certain grade to pass inspection. If not, it is subject to disciplinary action.

predominantly hands-on massage, many of these tools are quite instrumental in saving your hands from repetitive strain or injury when used occasionally. Some are also highly effective for trigger point therapy where deeper, pinpointed pressure may be needed. Be cautious with the use of tools on clients. They are not meant to be used over bony areas, and client comfort should be adhered to as much as possible. Check frequently with your client to make sure you're not applying too much pressure, using the tool for too long in one place, or using tools more often than the client would prefer.

Hot stones are also a favorite among many clients and most massage therapy training programs teach at least an introductory course on how to perform hot-stone massage. For this type of therapy special stones that retain heat as well as heating equipment are necessary. Hot-stone therapy is especially useful in colder temperatures and benefits not only the client, but the hands of the practitioner as well.

Bolsters and Pillows

These are important when considering client comfort. Oftentimes a body part may be better supported with the use of special massage bolsters or standard bed pillows. Support is essential for elderly clients, pregnant women, and people with certain illnesses that restrict their ability to lie face down or flat on their back. Massage bolsters are specially shaped cushions with leather or leather-like fabrics for easy cleaning and sanitation. They are quite durable and useful for differing client needs. Because of the sanitation aspect, these may be optimal for clinical use but are not as inexpensive or as versatile as standard bed pillows. Zipping bed pillows in barrier-style pillowcases is a practical idea to reduce allergens.

Audio System and Music

Though not considered essential, a decent sound system can provide wonderful ambience to a massage session. There are many types of ambience music dedicated to massage and bodywork sessions, but consider that the type of music suitable for one client may not suit another client's preferences. Keep a good supply of choices on hand. Music assists with covering outside noises as well as being relaxing. Many therapists may use nature sounds instead of music, which is also subject to preference. Note that water-related sounds make some clients feel the need to urinate and so may not be the best option during sessions lasting an hour or more. Always ask, and respect, a client's preference for what they want to listen to during a massage and remember that oftentimes they won't tell you unless you ask.

Lighting

Your home office will likely have adequate ceiling lighting but also consider muted-lighting sources such as lamps with shades or uplighting sources. These provide dim lighting that may be helpful in allowing a client to relax more fully than the light from traditional ceiling fixtures. Because a client may be lying on his back for at least a portion of the session, downward lighting cast over the table is seldom a good option unless it operates on a dimmer switch. Better to have an inexpensive table lamp off to one side than light that shines in a client's eyes in a supine position.

Air Quality

Depending on where your location is, air quality may need improvement. Air purifiers, fans, air-conditioning, and possibly a space heater may be desired to create a more comfortable atmosphere for you and your clientele. Always bear in mind that what is comfortable for you, as the practitioner who is moving and working around the table, is not always comfortable for the client lying on the table in various states of undress. Though the client is adequately draped with a sheet and blanket if needed, her body will cool as she relaxes in an unmoving state. The addition of air-conditioning for your comfort may not be conducive to her comfort level. A quiet room-size air-purifying unit should always be a consideration in a home-based massage practice where pets live even if they don't have access to the massage space itself.

Towel Warmer

A towel warmer is an extra feature worth investing in at some point. Clients most definitely appreciate the use of warm towels especially during the cold winter months. Because a client's body temperature drops during massage, warm towels can be especially pleasant on the feet or back. Electric towel warmer units come in boxed styles or as bars that can be wall mounted. Some retail houseware departments have towel warmers that are built for light to moderate use. Units for massage, physical therapy, chiropractic, or other therapeutic use typically have a more industrial construction designed for heavier use. Consider purchasing such an item through a massage supply company for maximum durability.

Hot or Cold Packs

Hot and cold packs can be gel- or herb-filled and are beneficial for anything from soothing aches and pains to reducing swelling. Most are easily microwavable or freezable and are much appreciated by a client with muscle or joint pain in a therapy session. There are also electric heating pad options, but beware of the safety factor with the use of such products. Herb- and grain-filled heating pads that you make yourself or purchase wholesale make a great item to sell in your practice. These can also be given as gifts for client referrals or for other special occasions.

Table-Warmer Pad

A table warmer is essentially a big electric heating pad. Extremely useful for encouraging a client's muscles to relax more readily (making your work easier), the table-warmer pad does double duty in providing real comfort to your client. For colder climates, these are an added incentive for current clients to book sessions because they know they will be comfortably warm throughout the session even without clothing on. Table-warmer pads come in different styles that cover the majority of the top surface of the massage table and are usually operated with a digital control for temperature, and for setting the time of operation. The warmer pad is designed with coils built into the material for even heat distribution. Most table warmers shut off automatically to reduce fire hazard but it's wise to check to make sure the one you choose has this feature.

Pain Relievers

Topical pain relievers are a good choice to have on hand for a massage session involving pain or strain for a client. Topical preparations come in creams, lotions, and ointments. Always check with a client for sensitivities they may have to ingredients in the product as many pain relievers applied to the skin contain ingredients that can cause irritation. Very often a massage practitioner will use a natural, organic product. It's an easy oversight not to ask the client if they have any sensitivity when using all-natural products, yet many of these preparations contain herbs that have allergenic ingredients for some people. Play it safe and always ask.

What Are the Essentials?

Whether you provide in-office massage, on-site, or both, the most important piece of equipment you will purchase is the massage table or chair. Many new practitioners will purchase their table while in school and an instructor typically will advise them on what to look for in a quality table. Talking to other practitioners or suppliers is another good way to determine the massage table or chair (or both) that will be most useful for your practice, based on your physical size, the space you'll be working in, the maximum projected size of your typical client, and other factors. An important note: The typical table purchased for use in massage school will commonly be inexpensive, relatively lightweight, portable, and easily set up and taken down. This option is ideal for school use but may not suit your further needs once you have graduated and received your license to practice.

There are many cheap massage tables and chairs now on the market, and these can be found in some retail establishments but more frequently on the Internet. Auction sites and international websites are readily available places to find these lower-quality tables and massage chairs, but be forewarned: The trade-off is frequently decreased quality in terms of the types of materials used, degree of comfort, and their ability to stand up with heavy use. Many reputable massage distributors also carry table lines that are mildly to very expensive. Most of these suppliers carry the majority of their stock in the moderately priced range and many of them carry product lines made with eco-friendly material, which may be a deciding factor for many practitioners. Because the massage table is the most important investment in the massage profession, the best advice is to invest in the best quality table or chair that addresses your needs yet remains within the budget you have set.

Beyond the massage table and chair, you will require table coverings and massage lubricants. A table or massage chair, linens, and lubricants alone can give you your start in the home-based massage business. This is great news if you're on a very limited budget.

As you begin to grow your business, you will be able to gradually expand your equipment and supplies base to include some of the other items listed to suit your increasing needs. As the massage field grows, so does the variety of computer software and other tools, equipment, and products that can make a practitioner's work easier.

Moving Forward

You've laid the basic foundation. You know whether you can own a home-based business in your locale and if so, the legalities of operating that business in your state, county, and city. You've honestly assessed your ability to own and conduct your home-based massage therapy business and you know the advantages and disadvantages that may come from doing so. You also understand the basics of designing a home-massage office and what to include in your business plan whether you wrote one for your own business and personal use or one that was generated for bank-lending purposes. And finally, you have determined what essential massage equipment and supplies you need immediately, and those you can hold off from purchasing or leasing until your business gains momentum.

So where do you go from here? Now it's time to dig deeper and make sure you have the following in place to further strengthen the foundation for planning the most successful start to your home-based massage therapy business.

Massage Education and License to Practice

This is probably an assumed fact, but nonetheless, a standard five-hundred-plus-hour massage therapy training program with the accompanying state licensing is a must in most states and deserves mention. Some states still have no mandates whatsoever regulating the practice of massage therapy, yet all states that are regulated have their own requirements. If you plan to set up shop in your state and then transfer to another one, you must know what the laws are that govern where you're going.

As stated above, massage therapy education programs have a state-specified number of hours of hands-on training. Programs differ slightly in curriculum but most include all therapeutic massage applications, including deep-tissue massage, infant and pre-natal techniques, geriatric massage, on-site or seated chair massage, sports massage, anatomy, physiology and pathology, psychology, craniosacral therapy techniques, reflexology, shiatsu and acupressure, polarity therapy, business professionalism, and ethics. A number of other Western and Eastern modalities may be included depending on the individual school curriculum.

National certification is not required in all states, but the credentials of this certification are beneficial and are discussed in further detail in appendix B. Schools for therapeutic massage often base their curriculum on the standards set by the National Certification Board for Therapeutic Massage & Bodywork (NCBTMB).

Scope of Practice

Be familiar with the laws regarding massage licensing in your state, if there is any, and always stay within the scope of your ability to practice. First and foremost, this means you don't diagnose or treat illness. You're also not a counselor, chiropractor, or a physical therapist (unless you are licensed in those areas as well). It is normal

and to be expected that there will be times your clients will want to discuss their
personal issues. Very often they will be in your office for stress relief, and for many
people, talking it out with a trusted person is helpful. Active listening and referrals
to other professionals are both appropriate actions to take with a client who wants
to tell you about personal matters. However, refrain from giving advice unless it is in
direct correlation to the massage therapy you are providing. And if the subject matter is inappropriate to the massage work environment or makes you uncomfortable
in any way, it is equally appropriate to explain that it is not an acceptable discussion.
Always conclude such discussions in a positive manner. You never want to make a
client feel chastised for sharing situations or their emotions with you, yet following
your business and personal boundaries are essential in maintaining a professional
client-practitioner relationship.

Another area of misconception is that many people think massage therapists
also give chiropractic adjustments. Unless you are also licensed to perform spinal
manipulation, it is not in your scope of practice as a licensed massage therapist to do
so. Why many clients have this mistaken belief is because, very often, when muscles
release their tension through massage therapy, the spinal vertebrae will spontane-
ously move back into natural position and the client will feel or hear the stereotypical
"crack" or "pop" that they experience in a chiropractor's treatment room. Frequently
a client will exclaim, "I didn't know you do adjustments." This is an important time

to remind them that you don't and to further educate them on how the muscles and bones work together.

Your state massage board dictates what type of bodywork modalities and treatments you can use, though there is some flexibility and overlap between the different health and wellness professions, as in the case with massage, chiropractic, and physical therapy. A clear example of this is all three professions utilize stretching techniques for clients. A definition of massage therapy is soft-tissue manipulation with the use of manual therapies to elicit normalization of those bodily tissues. Because stretching techniques fit under the heading of soft-tissue manipulation, they are entirely appropriate for your use as a massage therapist.

As a practitioner, you simply need to know what your state licensing board deems conducive to massage therapy and employ the options suitable and reasonable for you to use within the scope of your practice. Much of this will be taught to you in school, but as your business grows it is up to you to be aware of all current and changing regulations governing the massage therapy profession.

Stay within the bounds of your state's licensing regulations when you conduct your business and make sure that you have the appropriate training in any massage or bodywork modalities that you make claim to. Following these basic premises significantly reduces the risk of any actions on your part that may result in disciplinary measures being taken against you or the possible loss of your massage license.

Location, Location, Location

It's a well-known fact that most businesses that thrive are in a good location. In fact, it's probably fair to say that the location of your practice is not only important but can also make or break your business.

Businesses with great locations are generally easily accessible by car or foot, have good to excellent parking, are conveniently located in areas where there are a lot of people in their target market, and have other businesses around them that draw traffic.

Service businesses like massage therapy are especially dependent on where they're located because of the simple premise that they require people to actually come in to the facility. Optimally, a massage therapy location has other service businesses like hair salons, natural food stores, or chiropractor's or doctor's offices nearby.

Location, however, presents a challenge for the home-based massage therapy entrepreneur because a number of practitioners will have homes that are located in strictly residential areas, not commercial.

Residential Living

A service-oriented business ideally will be where people are and preferably in your target market. Let's face it, if you live one hundred miles outside of civilization, you may be hard pressed to get enough business to survive, let alone excel. If you live somewhere other than in a city, you'll need to honestly assess whether you can realistically generate enough clientele to maintain a home-based operation. You may need to supplement with a mobile operation doing on-site work as well to meet the monetary goals you have set for your business.

Apartment Dwelling

Other factors such as apartment living may have situations that are out of your control. Noise factors are common in heavily populated areas and in apartments where multiple families may reside. Apartments may not be adequately insulated to prevent or reduce the distraction of outside noise. Sound reduction may be an additional cost to you as the business owner to incur. And that's if the property owner even allows you to make physical alterations to the rental. If your local regulations allow a massage therapy business to be conducted from your apartment, consider doing some research on how to adequately reduce outside noise with sound proofing that stays within the parameters set by both your landlord and your economic means. Use the Internet as a free resource to research sound-deadening or sound-proofing measures. There you will find everything from options constructed with free materials to high-end, specially designed equipment or building materials that may be relatively costly.

Other Challenges

Think about parking issues or stairs and other access options that may be limiting for pregnant women, the elderly, or those who are physically challenged. If you restrict your massage practice to those who are young, healthy, and fit, you also severely limit your potential to serve your community and earn a viable income.

Because having a home-based business is generally considered "accessory use"—meaning the home is used as a business in addition to residential living (primarily residential not business)—handicap accessibility is unlikely to be required. But because all municipalities have different guidelines, it is important to contact your city or town clerk to determine if you are required to have handicap accessibility in your home or apartment. If so, you may incur greater renovation costs than you originally thought.

Some of these requirements may include handicap parking, a wheelchair ramp, widened doorways and hallways, and handicap-accessible toilets. For medical massage a stationary electric-lift massage table is useful for those clients unable to access standard tables. It is important to state in all business literature and other communications whether or not your home-based massage therapy business is handicap accessible or not (if not required by state or local law).

Foot traffic is another possible issue. If you're located in a rural area, you likely won't get many "off the street" clients. Walk-in customers are considered important to many service- and product-oriented businesses, so whether or not your home is strategically located to provide that additional avenue of business is worth examining. But because most massage practitioners schedule clients in advance, this may not be an issue of importance.

Start-Up Costs

Determine what you need for equipment and supplies, home renovation materials and labor costs, and licensing and regulation fees, then make a list of what your start-up costs will be. Use the "Start-Up Costs Worksheet" on page 56 to help you get started. Because you are starting your practice in your home environment, start-up expenses may be relatively low. Remember, to get started most economically in a home-based massage therapy business, you only need the three bare essentials (beyond any insurance costs and state or city fees): a massage table, linens, and lubricants. You likely already have these from school, so start-up costs needn't be overwhelming to the financially challenged.

Once you've created your list, use it as a starting point to determine your monthly budget. Include any other utilities, equipment, and expenses particular to your circumstances. Keep in mind that the start-up costs will differ from your operational expenses. There are initial costs such as basic equipment and furniture that will only need to be purchased once. After that, though there may be maintenance fees involved (such as needing a computer fixed), the operational-expense budget should remain fairly consistent with only minor fluctuations periodically.

Item	Estimated Cost
Licenses/Permits	
Office Supplies	
Remodeling/Decor	
Business Phone	
Business Checking Account	
Professional Membership	
Insurances	
Massage Equipment	
Massage Supplies	
Other	
Total	$

Insurance Needs

Because business-related insurance costs can be substantial, it's critical to be aware of the main types of coverage required, and determine what best suits your personal and business needs. Discussing your options with one or more insurance providers makes sense.

- **Homeowner's insurance (or apartment dweller's, if applicable):** Go over your policy carefully to determine liability coverage. Most likely, it is a standard policy that provides coverage for incidental guests in your home but not business clientele.
- **Major medical:** Commonly referred to simply as health insurance, this is a major insurance expense that you likely already have in place to provide coverage for medical expenses due to accidents or illness.
- **Disability insurance:** If you are the head of household or primary income provider for the household, disability insurance is a must have. Disability covers loss of wages in the incidence of accidents or illness that prevents you from working. The amounts paid out are determined by whether the disability is long or short term.
- **Liability insurance:** Liability covers accidents to business-related clientele who are injured while on your property. Never assume that your homeowner's will also cover business clients. Check with your insurance provider to be sure of what your coverage entails. If homeowner's insurance doesn't cover it, you will need liability insurance to cover medical expenses for a client's injuries and protect you against possible lawsuits resulting from those injuries. Most major governing massage organizations provide liability insurance. These organizations are listed in appendix A.

Business Image Projection

What kind of image do you want to project? This also relates to the studio versus office image. Ask yourself what massage therapy style you offer, or plan to provide in the future, and what type of image comes to mind when you think of your work. Visualize working in your ideal massage space with the optimal number of clients you want to see in your practice each day or week. See yourself actually working with each person in whatever capacity you may have chosen. The bodywork you offer may be for wellness-maintenance purposes, therapeutic massage for post-injury care, or to balance clients' busy lives with stress relief. Envision yourself starting and ending your day. See the payments you receive for your services and the expression on a client's face when they leave your office.

What will you teach your clients and, in turn, what will they teach you? What is the ultimate purpose of your dream? Take note of your vision, mission, and value statements and pull them together to formulate a picture in your mind of the business image you want to present.

Using these thoughts and questions to design the professional image you intend to project will be important when it comes to explaining what you do to prospective clients. Knowing what to say when someone asks what you do should be under the acronym that I have altered slightly: KISS, which for me means "keep it simply short." When someone asks what you do, if you just say, "I'm a massage therapist," generally you'll get a response of "Oh." Yes this is short and simple but it doesn't generate any interest from a person who could be a potential client either. It's WHAT you are, a massage therapist, not what you DO. On the other hand, if you say something like, "I facilitate healing in the soft tissues of the body to promote balance and well-being," though it is in fact true, the average person isn't going to be able to relate to it and you'll likely still get a response of "Oh." Be clear on what you do by visualizing very clearly the image you want to project, then learn to articulate what you do to others.

The business image you design will be further projected in the literature you create through business cards, brochures, and other marketing materials. Regardless of your massage style or dream practice visualizations, there are aspects that are "musts." These include generating a professional look for your home office and yourself, and conducting your business in a professional manner. Cleanliness, a comfortable ambience, privacy, punctuality, and confidentiality all play important parts in the image that your business, and you, will project. These, and others, will be discussed in greater depth in chapter 9.

How Strong Is Your Foundation?

Round out the big picture as you create your business from the ground up. I emphasize a really strong foundation of getting the minute details on legal issues, business start-up costs and budgeting, fairly assessing the home location and environment you will work from, and professionalism, professionalism, professionalism. But as with attending to the mundane issues listed above, it's equally important to dream and dream big! Visualize all that you want your practice to be. Realize that your visions will change as your business, and you, grow. Dream setting is an evolving process. And it's not only acceptable for your dream business to change, but it's inevitable because change itself is constant. As you dream and create your ideal massage practice, be realistic. Don't envision yourself seeing ten clients per day five days a week at an hour each. If it's even possible, it's also likely unsustainable for the long term. Follow the SMART plan when you visualize so you can bring the dream to fruition (see page 29).

Once you have your envisioned business image projection so distinctly detailed in your mind that you can see it clearly, learn to verbalize what you do. This ability to tell potential clients exactly what you provide is a major part of marketing yourself and your business.

If you don't have the appropriate skills for any of the massage techniques or modalities you want to employ in your practice, learn the skills you need to use them proficiently. And if you provide any type of counseling service, or other types of therapy that require additional licensure, make sure you have it before including it in your massage therapy practice.

Further, to have a successful business you must fully understand the massage laws that govern the state, city, or county where you practice to avoid disciplinary procedures and actions against you should you fail to operate within your scope of practice.

Much of this may seem like common sense and more than a bit boring to have to deal with, but just as a house built on sand cannot withstand crashing waves, neither can your business stand without adequate forethought and attention to the details of your dream and planning phases. Like with any business you start, going into it with blinders on can sink your business before it ever gets started.

06

Plan for Financial Success

Whether you're a new massage practitioner or a seasoned one, looking at the financial perspective is a key element to any successful business endeavor. Initially, there is much to be done in the form of organizing your finances to accommodate start-up costs and operational expenses, determining what types of payments to accept, assessing the feasibility of insurance reimbursement, fee setting, acquiring business loans if necessary, and setting up business accounting and banking practices.

Planning your finances means organization, organization, organization. Let me say it again: Planning your finances means organization. Finances (along with location) and how they are handled can make or break your new, or existing, home-based massage therapy business. How you plan them initially can greatly impact how you manage them later on. Start off on the right foot and money management becomes much more simplified and organized, and will put you in a position to achieve the success you desire.

Start with a Wealth Mind-Set

What does being wealthy mean to you? Is it having a lot of money, good health, or a wonderful family life? Is wealth identifiable by how much or how hard you work? Being prosperous can mean all of these things and more depending on what your definition of wealth is. No matter how you personally define it, wealth begins with a certain state of mind. I mentioned previously a can-do approach and this is the launching point because it's an attitude that says, "If I can come up with the idea, I can also come up with the plan to make it happen." Part of this attitude is watching not only how you think, but what you say day in and day out. Two common phrases for people who work are "I hate Mondays!" or "I can't wait for Friday!" Your choice to complain about a bad economy, not being able to pay the bills, or making have-to statements like "I have to see five clients today" instead of "I get to see five clients today" are all part of a language that takes you away from a wealth mind-set instead of toward it.

These types of thoughts and statements, when used frequently, become habits that are hard to break. Another consideration is to pay close attention to those people with whom you are in regular contact that may also speak negatively on a regular basis.

- Instead of "obstacle" think "challenge"
- Instead of "I should" think "I will"
- Instead of "maybe" think "yes"
- Instead of "I want to" think "I'm going to"
- Instead of "try" think "succeed"

Focus on the potential for achievement, not fear of failure, and use the language of the successful to bring your definition of wealth to reality. Fill your mind and your life with positive thoughts, statements, and actions to develop a wealth mind-set.

Keeping Costs Low

Many people who start any type of home-based business do it for the freedom of working for themselves. However, too often they find that the costs to start or do business are too high and their resources too low.

A massage therapy practice is a unique opportunity because being service-based provides very low initial start-up costs. And the reason many massage therapists choose a home-based practice to start with is because they want to save money. Providing massage out of your home certainly puts more income in your pocket. Without the overhead of renting or leasing space, travel expenses, and other costs, a practitioner can effectively make more money and actually be able to charge clients less, which is a win-win situation for both. So how do you go about keeping costs as low as possible without sacrificing quality?

New or Used

Initially, go through the list of equipment and supplies and determine which are essential to your business and which can be added as the business grows. The reality is if you work in your home office, you need a massage table, linens, some massage lotion or oil, and maybe some music to create ambience. Really. That is all that is crucial to providing massage from an equipment and supplies standpoint. If you do on-site massage at clients' homes or businesses, then you might need to include a massage chair to the essentials. The great part is these few items can be purchased for as little as around $500.

For used equipment you may pay even less and for new, higher-end equipment you'll pay more. Used equipment can be found on Craigslist and other online swap-and-sell sites. Check your local newspaper's classified ads for equipment you can get at a fraction of the price of new, or contact the massage school you attended that may have postings of used equipment. For a pretty minimal investment you can have a massage business up and running even in tight financial circumstances. Do a complete check of any used equipment you buy to make sure it's safe and sturdy before you spend your money.

Design Your Own Literature

Save costs by making good use of a home-computer system. A home computer can be invaluable for creating your own business literature. All it requires is a word processing and graphics program to type up your business information and add images, paper products such as business card stock and quality brochure and letterhead paper, and a printer. Printing your own business literature can be fun, creative, and economical in comparison to paying a printing company to do the work for you. In addition, the computer serves a dual function: design your business literature, and do your own record keeping—from accounting to client note taking. As your business grows you may want to investigate the possibility of paying other professionals to do these jobs for you. But there's no better way to save the expense than by taking the time to learn to do them yourself using your own computer and easy-to-use software.

Dress for Success?

Good news: Designer labels aren't required in the massage office. Nor do you need medical scrubs or massage logo shirts. Clothing requirements are typically the Three Cs of the massage profession: clean, comfortable, and casual. Short-sleeved shirts and khaki-style pants are a standard in manual therapy professions though, of course, there are many variations of clothing style you can wear. Consider the facts that long-sleeve shirts can get in the way of performing massage with your forearms and showing cleavage with V-neck style or low-cut tops on women practitioners may well be considered unprofessional by many people.

Because you work from home and not in a spa or clinical setting, there's no need to invest in uniforms or specialty massage clothing from a supplier when money is an issue. There's plenty of time for those later if you want them when you've reached your pinnacle of success.

Setting Fees

To know what to charge a client is a bit more of a challenge than just going by the current market rate in your area. There are other considerations to think about besides what others are charging. Yet knowing the area market is a starting point and you should begin with gathering information about what other practitioners with similar practices are setting for fees.

Many practitioners will set their fee structure with the intent to have their services affordable to everyone. This viewpoint is logical to the massage therapist who came into this profession to help people. Because of this very caring attitude, a practitioner will very often set her rates far too low in order to get as many people through the door as possible. Although this is a noble intention, setting fees too low may, in fact, deter business because of the mind-set that many people have that inexpensive means lower value or quality. Another point to consider is the one that will impact whether your business will survive or not. This is the reality: If you charge

Sample Service Fee Structure

30-minute Swedish massage: $35
60-minute Swedish massage: $60
90-minute Swedish massage: $85

30-minute salt glow back treatment: $45
30-minute salt glow add-on back treatment (when added to 60-minute Swedish massage for total of 90 minutes): $100

60-minute hot stone massage: $75

Seated chair massage: $1 per minute (minimum 10-minute session)

less, you will work more. The more hours you have to work, the more risk of burnout in a profession already statistically fraught with a high burnout rate. You must ask yourself if you can pay your expenses if you charge a lower-than-competitive fee for your services. Can you realistically work more hours physically? Massage is rigorous work and being fit enough to do the job is critical.

Thus, finding a balance between charging enough to sustain and grow your business, and not overcharging and driving potential clients into another therapist's office is your ultimate goal. It's something you may need to alter as necessary with time and experience.

Discounts

Other factors to consider in fee setting include discounting prices for clients who schedule frequently, sale prices for massage sessions, and gift certificates or product purchases for holidays, birthdays, and anniversaries. Some practitioners also offer senior-citizen discounts or sliding-scale rates to low-income clients. Discount pricing or specials give you a reason to stay in touch with clients who appreciate the occasion to save money and allow you to help more people. When discounting is used effectively, it can be a great marketing tool. But regardless of why you do it, it's important to remember that discounting will ultimately affect your bottom line either by lowering the amount of income generated or by forcing you to work more hours to maintain a desirable income-to-expense ratio. Keep balance in mind as you offer sales and other promotions or you may find yourself working that much harder for the same

Real-Life Story

A ninety-year-old client once advised me not to have the perpetual sale going on for my massage practice. I highly respected this person and listened to her intently as she explained that frequently offering discounts on my massage sessions would make people feel like they could simply wait for the next sale to schedule a massage. I found that wisdom invaluable throughout those early years of my practice—even though she concluded the conversation by asking when I was going to be having a special again because she wanted to buy several gift certificates for her family when I did.

amount of money you would have made had you'd charged your standard fee and provided massages to fewer people.

No-Show Fees

And then there is the subject of what is typically referred to in the massage profession as the "no-show." The no-show is the client who schedules a massage session then doesn't show up or call to say she won't be able to make her appointment. Unlike other health-related service businesses where three people may be scheduled for the same time slot, a massage session is scheduled for that one client. When she doesn't arrive for her session, you lose money in the form of the hourly rate she would have paid had she come in. Some home-based practitioners may let this practice go and simply fill that time with household chores (a benefit to the home-based operation), while others will charge a no-show fee, which is typically half to full price for the time reserved. This charge can be communicated to the client when scheduling her next appointment or by mailing them a bill with the fee listed. It's best to have a policy in place that specifically defines your expectations of a client with regards to arriving late, or not at all, for the scheduled session. This saves time, money, and headaches.

Business Checking Account

With having a home-based massage therapy business, you may be tempted to simply use an existing personal checking account to avoid having to pay a monthly fee for a business account. Don't. It's easy to say that you can separate business from personal income and expenses with careful balancing. It may seem even easier with online banking access at your fingertips. However, it takes very little to confuse and blur the line between what money is coming in and going out for business and what is going in and out for personal use. From a tax perspective this can be a nightmare and it is highly recommended by any tax professional for any business, home-based or not, to set up a business-only checking account. This way, you know exactly what is happening with funds deposited or drawn from that account at any time. Reconciliation of the account is far easier than if you combine the two.

The same can be said for credit card usage. If the rates and benefits are advantageous, consider getting a credit card through your banking institution. The benefit is you know your bank and your bank knows you. Any discrepancies on your credit card account can often be handled more easily than random credit card companies you may do business with. Whatever credit card company you use, be sure to use this card solely for business purposes. Many types of expenditures can be tax write-offs, so keeping business separate from personal is very important when it comes time to report income and expenses.

Insurance Reimbursement

Insurance reimbursement remains debatable among massage providers. Many insurance companies still do not consider massage as a viable health-care modality though more are leaning in that direction. With massage training also focusing more and more on preventative use and emphasizing education on massage benefits for many health conditions and injuries, insurance companies are beginning to sit up and take notice. As a plus many businesses recognize the importance of well-being programs that promote preventative measures such as exercise, diet, and stress relief, and set up flexible health-and-wellness plans that reimburse employees for money spent on certain wellness options.

Because massage is well known for relaxation and stress relief, it is becoming more identifiable as a wellness option that may be, in part or fully, insurable by some insurance companies. It may be a good idea to have your clients check with their workplace to find out if massage therapy is a covered benefit. (Do this only if you plan to accept insurance clients in your business.) Not only do preventative-wellness choices make sense in keeping consumers healthy, they also keep a healthier bottom line for insurance providers who may pay less in consumer claims. In many areas, massage is not covered for reasons considered unnecessary by a licensed medical practitioner or for preventative use, but this practice is changing as more employees and other health insurance consumers request CAM (complementary and alternative medicine) services such as acupuncture and massage therapy.

Now that the economy seems more like a roller coaster ride these days than a quiet drive down a country lane, the prospect of taking insurance payments may seem like a compelling option. However, as with most things in life, jumping in head first without knowing what lies ahead is seldom advisable.

Advantages of Insurance Reimbursement

■ An increase in clientele is the No. 1 reason most practitioners will provide insurance billing. I know I would be independently wealthy without ever doing massage again if I got paid for every person who simply asks whether

massage is covered by insurance. It stands to reason that with injuries, accidents, job-related incidents, and stress (which accounts for a substantial
percentage of health-related doctor visits per year), you could probably fill
your practice with insurance and worker's compensation clients alone if the
majority of insurance providers covered therapeutic massage.

- Contact with other health-care providers that can refer clients to you for
massage therapy. Essentially, this is a simple form of marketing that requires
networking with these providers and letting them know you accept insurance patients. When they have a patient with certain conditions that indi-
cate massage therapy might be beneficial, the health-care provider has your
name and contact information to refer the patient.

Disadvantages of Insurance Reimbursement

- Insurance billing is time consuming. Whose time? Your time. There's the
time it takes to discuss with a client the details of their health coverage.
Then there's the client-care notes that include a viable plan of treatment
you must accurately keep and the claim forms that must be submitted to
the insurance provider. You must be knowledgeable about the CPT codes
(current procedural terminology) that change frequently because they
must be posted on the forms you send in for reimbursement of services.
Beyond all of this, there is the possibility of needing to appear as a witness
in court litigation. Combine it all and there's a huge time commitment in
taking insurance clients. Only you can determine if the increase in income
outweighs the time commitment.

- Insurance companies decide what portion of the bill they will reimburse you
for. Because you bill one hundred dollars for a one-hour treatment does not
mean that's what the insurance company will approve and reimburse you
for. For instance, if you choose to participate as a network provider for a PPO
or HMO, you will be reimbursed a set fee and cannot bill the client for the
remaining amount. If you are a non-network provider, you may then bill the
client for the remainder of the fee.

- Some insurance companies take a long time to reimburse a provider. In
some cases, this can mean weeks, months, or longer. Following the referring
physician's prescription, keeping accurate client treatment notes, and using

the correct forms and current billing CPT codes will help smooth the path for successful payment.

Only you, the practitioner, can decide if accepting insurance clients will be profitable for you. It's a good idea to check with other massage providers in your area if this is something you think you may be interested in doing. See what their experience has been with insurance billing and act accordingly. Investigate it well because filing the forms incorrectly or with the wrong CPT codes can mean the difference between getting paid or having the claim denied and not getting paid. Also realize that all insurance companies are different, so ideally you will want to have your client find out the particulars with their insurance carrier before you provide massage services.

Acceptable Forms of Payment

You're not only in the massage therapy profession to help people, you're also in it to make a living or use it as a supplemental income. Traditionally, the massage profession has been a cash-oriented business. Even today, a client will most often pay in cash or with a check. Cash is good (and trust me, as a practitioner you will enjoy its benefits versus dealing with bounced checks or credit-card processing fees), but remember that the more forms of payment you accept the more convenient it is for your clients, which will, in all likelihood, increase business for you.

Becoming a Network Provider

Contact your state's insurance governing board or individual insurance companies to find out if CAM (complementary and alternative medicine) practitioners or, specifically, massage therapy practitioners are recognized as qualifying providers in your state. Washington State is one that does but most other states do not at this time. If massage therapy is recognized where you are, contact insurance companies that do enlist massage therapists as providers and ask about the rules and regulations that will govern your status as a health-care provider with them. You will be required to fill out the appropriate paperwork and adhere to their terms and conditions in order to receive reimbursement for your services.

Invoicing and Billing

The preferred method of payment for most massage therapists is payment received upon receipt of service. A practitioner must take the risk of being paid late or not at all when he provides massage to a client with the intent to bill them later. After all, once the service is rendered, there is no "returning" it if a client doesn't pay.

However, there will inevitably be times when an invoice may be required. Billing a client for services rendered or no-show fees (if applicable) can be as simple as designing and printing a simple invoice on your own business letterhead, then mailing a copy to the client while keeping a dated copy for your records.

Sample Basic Invoice

123 Eastern Drive
Any Town, NJ 00011
1(555) 555-5555

Client name:

Date of services:

Services rendered:

Payment due:

Payment due date:

Insurance Billing

Previously you learned about insurance reimbursement, which is one form of payment. Though it may be a viable way to increase the size of your massage practice, it may not be as lucrative as it seems at first. The best way to find out is by first determining your cost per client. Basically this is figuring out your month's expenses (business overhead) and dividing it by the number of clients you see in a month. Your result is what each client "costs." If your number is high, you may want to look at insurance billing as a way to lower client cost, which means more money in your pocket. Cost per client is difficult or impossible to determine if you are a new practitioner but works well if you have been in business steadily for nine months to a year.

The other way to determine if insurance billing is feasible for you is to talk to other area therapists as stated earlier. Find out who's doing insurance billing, how long the turnaround time for reimbursement is on average, and the workload involved.

Cash and Checks

Cash and checks are the dinosaurs of our technological age, but I don't know many service providers who don't have a love relationship with them. Other than potential issues with clients who may write a check for which there is insufficient funds from time to time, cash and checks are forms of payment that virtually guarantee you will receive full value. As a practitioner it is always wise to keep business cash separated from personal monies. As well, it is advisable to keep accurate records of cash payments just like recording checks or other forms of payment. The IRS will thank you. With cash payments, it is generally a good idea to supply a receipt for payment to the client with a duplicate for your files to avoid any possible questions about whether or not a payment was received.

When accepting checks, record the check number, amount, and date. This helps you to not only keep accurate records, but can assist the client who may ask for this information at a later date when they are reconciling a bank account. Always be aware of the potential for a client to bounce a check. Sometimes this is an innocent, one-time occurrence and sometimes it's a habitual issue. Decide your policy on bounced checks ahead of time and, if appropriate, let clients know of any charges they may incur by passing checks with insufficient funds.

The following sample receipt is shown as a two-part receipt. The left-side column is for the practitioner's records and the right-side column is the tear-off copy for the client. Two-part or duplicate-copy receipt books can be purchased inexpensively in

Date: From: For:	Date: Received from: For:
Amount paid: Amount due: Check #:	Amount paid: Provider signature:

stores that carry office supplies or you can produce and print your own on your business letterhead stock.

Money Orders and Cashier's Checks

Some people don't, or can't, have a personal checking account for whatever reason and may prefer to pay with a money order or cashier's check. These types of payments are secured (meaning when you cash them, there are available funds) and are perfect for clients who may frequently pay you with a personal check with insufficient funds to back it up.

The two forms of payment are similar in that they are both guaranteed because they are pre-paid. Money orders, unlike cashier's checks, can be purchased at stores and post offices. Anyone can purchase a money order and doesn't have to show any identification to do so. They must have the purchase price plus any fees associated with making the purchase transaction. Standard money orders are typically used for smaller purchases under a few hundred dollars. Postal money orders are available in larger denominations than what is typically allowed in grocery, drug, or convenience stores.

Cashier's checks, also known as bank checks, can only be purchased at financial institutions and are generally, though not always, used for larger purchases where a guaranteed form of payment is desired. Car purchases or down payments are examples where a cashier's check may be optimal. This form of check also has a handling fee that is paid at the time of purchase. To keep fraud to a minimum, many banks and credit unions may place a hold on cashier's checks for a period of up to two weeks until it clears the bank it was drawn on.

Credit- and Debit-Card Processing

Plastic is by far the most common way for most people to pay for anything these days. From gasoline to groceries, credit and debit cards are highly utilized by just about everyone, so it's a wise massage practitioner who decides to accept them in her home-based massage therapy business.

Initially, this may not be feasible. There are costs related to accepting credit and debit cards. You must have a merchant account with a processing company that will charge you an initial start-up fee, equipment lease or purchase fees, and a monthly fee. On top of that are transaction percentage fees. Unless you have a strong client base, it may not be advantageous to your business to accept credit and debit cards. If you have a client base that is growing, it's definitely time to start shopping around for credit-card processing options. It may be overwhelming at first because there are a lot of them out there. You can find them in big discount stores, at your local financial institutions, and in abundance online. Each one will claim to be the very best for your distinct needs. Only you can determine if this is true, so do your homework.

Processing companies offer everything from the manual swipe variety to terminals or wireless terminals. A plus for massage therapists in particular is there are also companies that can process payments through landline or cell phones, making it indispensable for those therapists who work at various on-site locations.

Computer credit-card processing is also worth mentioning. Because this may be a more costly option, this is typically for the more seasoned practitioner who has an established client base and wants to sell gift certificates, pre-paid massage sessions, or products through her website via an online shopping cart.

Is Your Financial Plan in Order?

Design your comprehensive plan for financial success. This includes coming up with creative ways to limit your initial cash outlay and determining what you really need to start your business with, while adding in other expenses as your business grows.

From here, it's more about looking at your goals and determining the number of clients you need to see per week or month to meet expenses and the monetary expectations you've set for yourself. Setting fees for your massage therapy services is an important factor in reaching these goals. Although it may seem prudent to under-cut your competition by pricing lower than area therapists, you may just find in the long run that it isn't the wisest choice. It's fine to offer start-up specials to introduce yourself, but keeping those lower rates may serve a negative dual purpose: 1) to give you a lesser perceived value to your clients, and 2) to make you work more hours to meet your expenses and reach the financial goals you've established.

Start your financial management off on a good note by separating your business and personal monies through separate bank and credit-card accounts. If you choose to pay yourself out of your business income, simply transfer earnings to your personal account and keep the remaining income in your business accounts to pay expenses.

Finally, investigate the advantages and disadvantages of accepting insurance reimbursement. For many therapists, it's a viable way to dramatically increase their client base. For others, it's more work than it's worth. Only you can decide if it can work for you and your practice. Keep in mind that the more forms of payment you accept, including insurance reimbursement, the more potential clients you may attract to your massage therapy business. Ultimately, multiple payment options may be worthwhile regardless of the challenges that each form may present.

Figuring Client Cost

If currently in business for a minimum of one year, add up your total business expenses for the year. If you're just starting up, use a projected business expense worksheet to calculate the total.

- Divide the year's total by twelve to get a monthly total.

- Add up the number of massage clients seen or projected for each month.

- Divide the month's expense total by the number of massage clients to get a per client cost.

Simply put, cash flow is the money that flows in and out of your massage therapy practice. It, more or less, is cyclical in nature in that you take in cash from your clients for the services you render, and then send it back out in the form of payment for bills to keep the business operational. You then receive more money from clients, pay money back out, and the cycle repeats itself over and over again. Ideally, for every dollar that goes out, one (or more) dollars comes back into the business in the same time frame, but often the timing of cash flow is slightly or substantially off. This means that more times than not there is a gap where more money may be going out than coming in. Projecting ahead for how much, and when, cash is being paid out and when it's due in will help keep you alert to any potential problems. Keeping your costs low, not offering the perpetual sale or discounted massages, budgeting, and accurate expense and income record keeping can all help narrow the gap.

Budget

Without a budget you won't know what money will be needed to meet your weekly, monthly, and incidental expenses. No rocket science here. Even if it's only a piece of paper listing your monthly outgoing bills due, you need something to go by, otherwise you'll quite possibly get to month's end without sufficient income to cover those bills. This, in turn, may leave you no choice but to dip into personal income to pay for business costs. Need I say this is never a good plan? So make sure you draw up some sort of budget to give you a reasonable idea of what your cash outlay is going to be, whether for weekly or monthly expenditures. Then use effective marketing to build or maintain your client base to, at minimum, earn what you need to meet expenses.

Realize that initially, you may have no idea what your expenses will be. This is the time to estimate. Try to overestimate versus underestimate so you don't lose income at month's end. It may not work out that way, but it's the standard to shoot for nonetheless.

Expenses will fall under these general categories:

- Utilities (electricity, phone, etc.)
- Supplies (laundry detergents, massage lubricants, linens, equipment, etc.)
- Loans (student, business)
- Taxes (property, income)
- Insurances (health, liability, disability)
- Professional services (accountants, marketers, etc.)
- Marketing (advertising, business stationery, Internet access, website design and hosting, etc.)
- Professional fees (license, membership, and continuing education)
- Miscellaneous

There will likely be other expenses not listed above. Simply add these other expenses to your own budget to make it accurate for your business. Also keep in mind that some fees and costs may not be weekly or monthly expenses. A state license, for instance, is a yearly expenditure. For those that are quarterly or yearly, simply divide the amount paid within a given year by twelve to get a monthly figure.

Paying Yourself

This topic is heatedly debated among business owners. Some people believe that all income earned should be put back into the business and others, myself included, believe that you should pay yourself too. In fact, I would challenge you to consider the idea of paying yourself FIRST. I can hear the gasping as you say, "I can't pay myself first! My bills ALWAYS come first. I'll pay myself after I pay the bills." Follow this creed and I guarantee there will be no money left to pay you at all at week or month's end. The reason for this is the premise that there will always be something else to buy or pay out on.

Think of it this way: If you have a J-O-B, you work for an employer, exchanging your time and effort for money. If you didn't trade your work for pay, you would be a volunteer and that's a different arena altogether. The income you receive for work rendered may pay for needs like housing, transportation, and other living expenses. It, in all likelihood, covers the items that fall under the category of "wants" too. It is probable that it pays for dinner out once a week, a family vacation, new shoes and clothes, or recreational items. If your boss didn't pay you, you couldn't have the wanted items—much less the needed ones.

Running your own home-based business is not much different from having a job other than that you are the boss and usually the workforce. You need an income to pay the bills, which will provide security, business growth, and success, but paying yourself (first) is what will give personal satisfaction and continued motivation to do what you do.

So how does it work to pay you first? When you first start out in your massage therapy practice, you may find there's more month than money when it comes time to pay bills. That's OK. Even if you can only pay for a cup of coffee, buy a cup of coffee. As your business grows, pay yourself more.

Initially, your motivation to grow your business may come from your deep desire to help people. This is great motivation, but it's not as long lasting as you might think. Massage therapy is a hands-on job that can physically and mentally burn out a practitioner sooner than she may anticipate. It's vitally important to remember key elements of self-care. And it is my opinion that paying yourself first is one of the keys to enjoying other things beyond work.

Expense and Income

Business expenses are the costs of doing business. They are what reduce your gross income to the net income you will be taxed on. Income, of course, is the money that flows into your business and it may come from several sources other than client sessions.

Accurate expense and income accounting is a necessary evil. We're massage therapists and most often that means we don't really want to do accounting. In fact, I dare say most of us don't want to do ANY paperwork. It's mundane, it's time consuming, and it takes us away from what we love, which is massage. Accounting and other record keeping places a reality check on a massage therapist's hourly rate as well. You may charge seventy dollars per hour for a massage, but add in daily, weekly, and monthly record keeping hours and your hourly rate of pay drops. Yet without it, tax time can be a nightmare.

Expenses

A very simple way to make your expenses easy to track is by keeping all receipts in a large envelope or accordion-style file. Mark on the outside of the envelope or file

(Any expenses that are paid yearly are divided by twelve to get the monthly cost.)

Expenses Monthly	Estimated Monthly Cost
Utilities	
Telephone/cellular	
Car for business use (gas, maintenance, insurance, payments)	
Insurance (liability, health, disability, etc.)	
Banking fees	
License/permit fees	
Loans (student, business)	
Taxes	
Product inventory (if any)	
Massage supplies	
Office supplies	
Marketing	
Maintenance, housekeeping, laundry	
Continuing education	
Salary/paycheck	
Total:	$

what each individual receipt is for, the date, to whom the money was paid, and how much the receipt total amount is. Writing the information down immediately will make sorting those receipts far easier when it's time to account for them on your taxes. Include vehicle service and gas receipts, entertainment or workshops that directly correspond to your business, office and massage supplies, advertising costs, clothing (that is used specifically for work), utilities, credit-card slips, and any other receipts that have to do with your home-based massage business. In addition, your accountant can help you determine what home costs you can include under your expenses.

Income

Recording your income can be as easy as writing down a client's payment at the time of service in your appointment book, if there is adequate space to do so. This is an easy habit to get into and can serve a dual purpose to remind you to book your client's next massage appointment. Simply write in the amount and type of payment. If the payment is by check, record the check number as well. This basic information can be transferred weekly or monthly to an income ledger or computer record-keeping program. Remember that if you sell products or gift certificates, these must also be recorded as gross income. As a service-based business, clients will often tip for massage therapy. Tips are considered income and must be recorded as such.

Barter

Many service providers will trade, or barter, services with other providers. This is acceptable in the eyes of the law but you must remain diligent about reporting these services even though no cash exchange may be involved. Though all municipalities may have their own rulings on bartering, in general, if massage therapy is exchanged for a deductible service like record keeping, then the massage is listed as income and the record keeping can be used as a deduction on your taxes. However, if massage services are exchanged for a personal service such as those offered in a hair salon, the massage service is considered income but the hair care is not a deductible service because it is considered personal, not business related. Keep this in mind when deciding whether or not to barter services with other area businesses.

When determining whether or not to barter, remember too that you could easily barter yourself out of a business cash flow. Yet when you manage the bartering option with a balanced approach, you could trade massage services for chores you

Name	Date	Service/Product Gift Card	Amount Due or Paid	Payment Type
Example: John Smith	10/01/12	1-hour massage	Pd: $65.00 +Tip: $5.00	Check # 4321
Total:			$	

Examples of Tax-Deductible Bartering Options

- Accounting

- Advertising

- Business consulting

- Carpentry

- Child care

- Cleaning services

- Computer assistance

- Laundering services

- Plumbers

- Printing services

- Transcription

don't like such as laundry service, accounting, or billing. In many cases you may still be bartering time for time, yet you are trading off those things you either don't do well or that you don't care to do yourself.

Something else to keep in mind is the benefit of bartering massage for massage. Bodywork is a rigorous job and it's important to take care of your physical and mental health. One of the best ways to take care of you is by getting the massage therapy that you recommend daily to your clients. Practice what you preach and use bartering to do so.

How Will You Manage Your Cash Flow?

Create a budget worksheet that specifically addresses your business needs. Use it to determine what you'll need to earn that month to meet your expenses. Your budget will be helpful each month to determine where you may need to cut back, or in the case of overbudgeting, where you can add in extra expenses that may be beneficial for your business such as continuing education. Keep in mind that initially your budget may show what are considered one-time expenses, or those that may not need to be purchased again immediately. These may include a massage table or other equipment that is necessary but generally considered as start-up expenses that won't be repeated soon.

Keep accurate records of your business expenses. This can be as simple as using a file folder or as complex as a software program for the computer. It may not be the fun part of your massage therapy practice but it's an integral part of doing business. If you don't know what money is going out, you're going to have a hard time sticking to any type of budget or even knowing the projected income you'll need to sustain your practice.

On the reverse, also record all of your income. This includes payments for massage therapy services, gift cards or certificates sold, retail products, and any services or products you barter with other area businesses. Only by recording all expenses and income generated can you accurately provide the data needed for your taxes.

Last, but hardly least, is the subject of paying yourself first. You can choose to put all income directly back into your business (and for a while you may not earn much), or you can start right from the beginning by giving yourself a paycheck. It is my opinion that paying yourself is not the last thing you should do, but indeed, it is the FIRST thing you should do. Watch your motivation to succeed soar even if paying you first means buying a fancy latte at the start.

Proper management of your money is essential to not only keep your business alive but help it thrive and grow into the success you want it to be. It's important not only to keep the cash flowing in and out of your business as fluidly as possible but also to know when there will be gaps and plan ahead for them through proper budgeting, and expense and income reporting.

08 Taxes and Record Keeping: Do I Have To?

As stated before, paperwork is the bane of existence for most massage therapists. We want to do the healing work we were trained to do, which is helping people relieve stress, heal from injury, and reach higher levels of wellness. Our goals are to impart relaxation and a strong sense of well-being in not only our clients but in ourselves. We start massage school with those thoughts and we end with those thoughts, even though basic tax information and record keeping is covered in the business portion of the curriculum. Yet no matter how extensive or in-depth the business part of our training is, our minds don't stay in taxes and record-keeping mode. They quickly revert back to the excitement of getting into hands-on massage practice. We delve into the discovery of muscles, how the body works, and how and why it malfunctions. Learning new massage techniques and bodywork modalities create an eagerness we can barely contain. Yet seldom do we spend sleepless nights with the burning desire to learn how to manage tax deductions, write client-care notes, or record expenses and income.

At the same time, although we don't want to do it, we know we have to take on the task because it's virtually impossible to sustain a business without also doing the business of keeping accurate records. The key then becomes figuring out a way to manage record keeping in the most efficient, yet least tortuous manner possible.

Client Documentation

Documentation begins with the information a client supplies before the first massage session they schedule. An individual file, whether manually kept or stored on the computer, should be kept for each client. This file should consist of intake forms, SOAP charting (to be discussed in this chapter), update notes, and other information about, or supplied by, the client. Though client record keeping can be extensive and monotonous, it's important to make it a daily habit. Depending on your memory to recall a client's information is unrealistic if you have a busy, thriving practice with a strong client base. It also looks much more professional to a client when a massage practitioner appears to remember her complaint, progress or lack of, and the plan to address her needs. Keeping abreast of a client's condition is a simple matter of looking at her file before her session.

Contact File

Though not necessary, a contact file is invaluable for having an easily accessible list of all clients, potential clients, and their contact information. In the past a typical way to keep a contact list, or file, consisted of using a Rolodex or index-card file box with clients' names, addresses, and phone numbers written on them and filed alphabetically. This is a still a perfectly acceptable standard and may be optimal for your needs.

However, with modern technology a PDA or cell phone has client contact information literally at your fingertips. With these types of devices you have only to input the information as you receive it and then save it in your address book. Most devices also have the capacity to store work addresses and phone numbers, and limited personal information such as birth dates, anniversaries, and short notations.

Contact information can also be stored on a computer, which is useful for sending e-newsletters or for printing standard mailing materials quickly and easily. Although electronic devices make storing client data more simplified, I also recommend you have a written copy in your files should something happen to the digital version.

Client Information (Intake) Form

Part of massage therapy school curriculum is learning how to take client notes, one of the first being the client information, or intake, form. This form varies from therapist to therapist. There are standard forms you can use or you can design one that best suits your needs. Information forms may be shorter in length for on-site massage sessions that are fifteen minutes or less in duration and longer and more detailed for standard massage therapy sessions of thirty to ninety minutes.

Shorter intake forms are less time consuming to fill out and more convenient for a client who you may only see once at an on-site location such as at a sporting event. If you plan to see a client more than once, the longer, more detailed form may be the better option.

Short intake forms may include minimal information such as basic personal information, complaint, medical conditions, if applicable, and a client signature section. A longer form will include space to input concerning health conditions, medical treatments, and medications. It may also ask about lifestyle conditions such as physical activity, stress, and water-intake levels. The typical information form will also include a section for a client to detail his particular complaint or reason for coming for massage therapy. Some forms have body diagrams so a client can circle the specific areas of complaint.

Both short and long client-intake forms should have a general informed consent section near the bottom stating that massage therapy is for the purpose of relaxation and relief of muscular tension or strain and should not be misconstrued as diagnosis or treatment of any illness or medical condition. It is also useful to include in this section that it is to be understood by the client that the massage session is for therapeutic purposes only and that all policies have been read and understood. If you design

Informed Consent Form

Because massage intake forms vary in content, the following is just a sample of what an informed consent section might look like:

All information I have provided is complete and accurate to the best of my knowledge. I understand I am responsible for notifying the massage therapist of any discomfort during the massage session and for any changes to the information given. I agree to hold him/her harmless if I fail to provide such notification. I further understand that massage and bodywork is for the basic purpose of reducing stress and relieving muscular pain and strain and is not to be considered medical diagnosis or treatment. I acknowledge that the massage provided is for therapeutic, non-sexual purposes only. I have read all policies regarding cancellations and late or missed appointments and agree to pay any fees associated with these policies.

Client Signature: _____ *Date:* _____
Parent Signature: _____ *Date:* _____

Client Information Form

Name: _____

DOB: _____

Address: _____

Phone number: _____

E-mail address: _____

Emergency contact: _____

How is your general health? (excellent, good, fair, poor)

Do you have, or are you being treated for, any medical conditions? ❏ Yes ❏ No

If yes, what? _____

Are you experiencing any areas of pain or discomfort? ❏ Yes ❏ No

If yes, where? _____

_____

Are you on any medications? ❏ Yes ❏ No

If yes, what? _____

Do you have allergies (in particular to scents or body preparations such as lotions)? ❏ Yes ❏ No

If yes, what?_____

On a scale of 1–10, what is your stress level? _____

How much water do you drink daily?_____

Have you had massage therapy before? ❏ Yes ❏ No

If yes, when? _____

How did you find out about our massage services?_____

What did you come in for today? (pain relief, stress/tension, relaxation, etc.) _____

_____

I understand that therapeutic massage is non-sexual and is for the basic purpose of inducing relaxation and reducing stress and strain. It should not be misconstrued as medical diagnosis or treatment. I have completed all information above as completely as possible and agree to hold the practitioner harmless if I fail to inform him/her of any changes in my condition. I further understand that if I arrive late, my session will end at the scheduled time in order to keep the practitioner on schedule for the next client and that missed appointments without a 24-hour cancellation notice may be charged the full fee.

Client signature: _____

Date: _____

your own intake form, be sure to include a place for parents or other responsible party to give consent for minor age children.

Therapists vary in their procedure for filling out the initial intake forms. Some prefer to ask the questions of the client and record the answers they give, while others simply let the client fill in the form himself. The advantage to filling the form out together is oftentimes the massage therapist can get more in-depth information on specific questions than if the client completes the form alone. The more detailed information a practitioner gets from the client the better service he can provide.

Also, some massage practitioners will have a separate intake and informed consent forms. This is personal preference dependent on what information you wish to include in each one.

SOAP Notes

With each client, it's important to take progress notes after each session. In clinical terms, SOAP stands for subjective, objective, assessment, plan. SOAP charting is the most commonly used form of recording a client or patient's information. SOAP charting is taught to, and understood by, the majority of health-care practitioners in most medical settings.

- **Subjective:** This is the preliminary discussion with a client about his symptoms, the intensity and frequency of those symptoms, and any activities and treatments that help the condition feel better or worse. When combined with information on the intake form, this presents a broader picture to a practitioner who will then observe the client.
- **Objective:** The objective section is to record practitioner observations and tests, which are combined with the client history and complaint to determine a plan and the goals for the massage session.
- **Assessment:** The assessment is a notation of what was done and the result or changes experienced by the client during or after the massage session. All progress, good or bad, is noted here.
- **Plan:** This section is for stretching, exercise, or other suggestions for the client for home use as well as a place to record suggestions for future massage therapy, including the number of sessions and how long each should last.

Client: _____

Date: _____

Subjective: _____

_____

_____

_____

_____

Objective: _____

_____

_____

_____

_____

Assessment: _____

_____

_____

_____

_____

Plan: _____

_____

_____

_____

_____

_____

_____

CARE Notes

Another form of record keeping potentially more accurate for massage therapy clients falls under the acronym CARE, which stands for condition, action, response, evaluation. Many massage therapists feel the CARE charting method is more applicable to massage where many clients come for wellness maintenance, stress relief, or other non-specific reason versus using SOAP charting, which is more useful with conditions for which there are specific symptoms and markers of progress to note.

- **Condition:** What the client tells you regarding what is going on with them. This area reflects what the client wishes to achieve, any particular body areas of concern, stress level, or anything else pertinent to why they are seeing you for massage.
- **Action:** Depicts any actions (specific type of massage, stretching, products) the massage practitioner utilizes to address the client's concerns. Here is also where you would note any client positioning or use of supporting bolsters.
- **Response:** What the results are or any differences from the client's original condition. This section should accurately report any changes, good or bad, that you or the client notice regarding the client complaint or goal for the session.
- **Evaluation:** The recommendation section for client homework or future sessions. The evaluation is optional but useful in forming a plan for the future when combining initial session goals and complaints with the palpable results and client response.

Client Updates

Client files should be kept up to date from month to month or more often if they receive frequent massage. Information kept in a client's update notes should be any alterations to contact information (cell phone numbers and e-mail addresses are frequently changed), changes in health, medication, or in the condition for which the client originally came to you. These changes should be updated frequently and reviewed before each session.

Make all client notes easily readable to someone else. In the case of SOAP or CARE charting for insurance or legal purposes, it is important for someone else reading your notes to be able to understand exactly what type of massage was provided, techniques used, and the specific results that were achieved. Use technical and

Client: _____

Date: _____

Condition: _____

_____

_____

_____

_____

_____

Action: _____

_____

_____

_____

_____

_____

Response: _____

_____

_____

_____

_____

_____

Evaluation: _____

_____

_____

_____

_____

_____

medical terminology (i.e., abdomen not stomach) whenever possible. It's fine to use shortened sentences as long as they still make sense in the context of the notation. There are no penalties for improper use of the English language so abbreviations and fragmented sentences are acceptable. However, it's still important to compose the note with the comprehension of the intended reader in mind.

Manual Bookkeeping

Manual bookkeeping is still a standard for many therapists. For client files it usually entails keeping alphabetically organized manila file folders in a file cabinet. When this type of filing system is employed, it is relatively easy to find a client's file when needed. The drawback is it doesn't take long to fill a filing cabinet once you begin really building your client base, seeing clients regularly, and writing intake, SOAP or CARE notes, and record updates. For the environmentally conscious, manual note taking leaves a footprint in the form of a tremendous paper trail so consider keeping digital records and reliable backup copies.

For recording income and expenses, the impact is not quite so much. A simple bookkeeping ledger is all that is required to keep accurate financial records. All information is contained within a single ledger and available with a turn of the page. Many massage supply companies offer bookkeeping ledgers with the specific categories most commonly used in the massage therapy profession. Remember that when noting revenue and expenditures, the information must be recorded as accurately and neatly as possible so that if questioned, the information is understood or explainable.

The manual method of record keeping is the least expensive option and is ideal for the practitioner just starting out, one who wants to save money, or one who simply likes the method better. With a busy massage practice, most practitioners will soon outgrow the manual method of pencil and paper and move on to input information on a computer.

For some people, a quicker way to manually keep records is to type them into a word-processing document then print and save them in a filing cabinet. This makes client notes far more legible and less time consuming to prepare.

Record-Keeping Software

Electronic financial documentation through record-keeping software can be as simple as using the software pre-installed on most home computer systems.

Depending on the scope and size of your practice, this may be all you need to keep accurate financial records. When combined with a word-processing program (also pre-installed), you can effectively keep all client and income and expense records without additional cost to you.

For those who wish to invest in more advanced software programs, there are many versions for both online and offline use that can record all facets of your business from appointment setting to client documentation and financial record keeping.

Offline Software

Offline record-keeping software is purchased and installed on your computer system. Like most software you put on your computer, each has certain requirements in terms of processor speed, RAM, and available disc space. The advantage to offline massage therapy record-keeping software is you pay one price and many companies offer free upgrades.

Offline software typically includes the following:

- Client scheduling calendar
- Client contact and personal information wizards and manager
- Massage session wizards and managers to record client notes
- Financial record keeper
- Product and gift certificate sales tracker
- Birthday, anniversary, and special occasion manager

Online Software

The biggest advantage to online software is you don't take up space on your hard drive with large files associated with your business. Online programs are exactly that: online. Typically, you subscribe to the software program on a monthly basis and sign in as needed. As with offline software, free updates are usually included with your subscription and all reports are printable.

Online software often includes the following:

- Client management sections with contact information, intake forms, and a record of the number of sessions
- Massage session manager including type of session, dates of service, and individual payments made or outstanding

- Gift certificate and product tracking with dates, types, and payments
- Expense manager
- Appointment manager

Taxes

On the subject of massage therapy taxation, a tax professional is going to be a very important asset. But even with an expert in your corner, as your own boss it's up to you to know the ever-changing tax laws in your state and adhere to them. You must understand how much tax you will owe, when taxes are due, expenses you can use as deductions, and those you can't. But just as not everyone knows the massage therapy profession the way you do, you likely do not know the intricacies of the tax field the way a tax expert would. Use any information here as a general overview of

Self-Employment Taxes

If net earnings from your home-based massage therapy business are $400 or more, you are required to file self-employment taxes with the Internal Revenue Service. Self-employment taxes are those that encompass Social Security and Medicare taxation.

Most self-employed individuals who expect to owe at least $1,000 in tax revenue will need to pay *estimated* self-employment taxes. These are due in quarterly installments. Estimated self-employment taxes are figured by using the IRS form 1040-ES, which can be found on the IRS website as well as local IRS offices and many post offices. Failure to pay on time or enough quarterly taxes can result in penalties.

Perhaps one of the bigger hassles of having your own business is the need to pay these self-employment (and other) taxes that would normally be taken care of by your employer. Yet there are many deductions that can be used to offset the taxation that you pay in as a business too. I can't emphasize enough the importance of utilizing the skills of your accountant to assist you in figuring out which tax laws pertain to your business to make sure you pay no more and no less than what you owe.

some helpful points, yet for the details work closely with a qualified tax professional. If costs are prohibitive consider using fair trade (barter) of massage therapy services to get the tax help you need.

Something to discuss with your accountant is your responsibilities regarding paying quarterly taxes. These taxes are an estimate and your accountant can help you calculate the amounts you will owe. Not filing or not paying quarterly may incur a penalty at the time you file your annual tax return.

Several often overlooked or misunderstood tax deductions are for vehicle, home office, travel, meals, and entertainment.

Vehicle Deductions

Most people realize that they can deduct vehicular costs on their income tax return. There are two ways to take this deduction: 1) actual car expenses, and 2) the standard mileage rate. Because there are benefits and drawbacks to each, and only you and your accountant can determine which deduction method is best for your situation.

I'm always surprised by how many people don't take deductions for vehicle usage. "It's too much work," "I can't remember to record mileage," and "I use my car for both work and personal, which makes it too confusing" are some of the excuses I hear. I agree those are all likely, yet it makes absolute sense to deduct this necessary expense as part of your overall tax strategy even if your primary workplace is home.

Keep in mind that if you deduct actual car expenses like gas, maintenance, insurance, and other costs in a given year, you cannot use the standard mileage rate in that same year.

Home-Office Deductions

The home office is also a confusing issue for many massage practitioners. There is a lot of gray area in what can, and cannot, be used for tax purposes. To avoid an IRS audit, it's critical to either research the facts on your own or discuss it with your accountant.

Deductible expenses may include but are not limited to the following:

- Insurance
- Mortgage interest
- Depreciation
- Utilities
- Home repairs

The requirements for qualification are that all or a portion of your home must be used regularly and exclusively for business purposes. An example for a home-based massage therapy practice is if you use an entire room or part of a room to conduct business from, it can be considered a deductible expense. To take the deduction you must first determine the percentage of your entire home that is used exclusively for business. The IRS has a publication that provides complete information on qualifying for home business deductions, including types of expenses, deductions for business equipment and furniture, figuring business percentages, home depreciation, and other applicable information on the business use of your home. The publication also includes worksheets and instructions on how to complete them. See appendix A for resource information.

Travel, Dining, and Entertainment

The laws are strict on what constitutes travel, dining, and entertainment for business use. As with home deductions, expenses related to these are only deductible if they are used for business-related purposes. If travel expenses are purely for business reasons, then the entire cost is deductible. Yet if portions of it are for personal use, those portions are not. For example if you travel to a five-day massage conference in Boston and three days are spent in workshops and the remaining two are used for sightseeing, then only the three days of business-related activity are income-tax deductible.

Entertainment, meals, and gifts are all only deductible when they are used for business as well. Keep excellent records of expenses as proof that they were incurred for business use. This includes keeping receipts for all expenditures such as hotel, dining, travel, and entertainment costs. Date and record what each receipt is for to support it as evidence if needed. A credit card used exclusively for this purpose also works well as proof.

Accounting and Tax Assistance

There are many options for gaining accounting or tax assistance including software and Internet websites. I cannot stress enough, though, the advantages of having a live professional in your corner even if only to advise you of new laws, credits, or deductions you can use for your business. If you ever have a tax complication arise, you will find her help invaluable especially in the case of an IRS audit.

- **Accounting software:** This software is generally comprised of different sections relating to accounting. These areas cover both money coming in (receivables) and money going out (payables). Accounting software is only as good as the person inputting the data.

■ **Certified public accountant:** A certified public accountant (CPA), simply put, is someone professionally trained in bookkeeping. This includes, but is not limited to, preparation or analysis of financial documents, audits, and providing advice on tax laws. An accountant may work within a larger firm or have a private practice.

■ **Tax attorney:** A tax attorney is a lawyer specializing in tax laws. A tax attorney is useful for handling legal issues concerning more complex tax matters. An accountant is the standard provider for your accounting business needs unless you are looking to change your business structure at a future date or you are faced with an investigation of tax fraud or other criminal activity.

■ **Internet access:** The IRS and SBA (Small Business Administration) offer free forms and publications on tax laws, deductions, and many articles on owning and operating home-based businesses. The IRS site also has access to tax help for people in need of low-cost or free assistance.

How Will You Stay on Top of Your Taxes?

You may not want to do it or you may even dread it. But there's no way around record keeping and taxes if you own and operate a business. Because you're the boss, it's your sole responsibility to make sure these are attended to whether you do them yourself, barter them out, or pay a professional to handle them for you. Neither one is a small chore and each will account for a sizable chunk of your time. The upside to either task is there is a multitude of options to help make the work load easier.

Small Business Administration

The SBA's sole focus is helping the small business owner to succeed. By providing business planning strategies, tools to attain financing, an extensive education library, and help to find local resources, the SBA becomes a one-stop shopping source for information and guidance in the start-up, growth, and management of your home-based massage therapy business. The SBA also works extensively with particular groups, such as veterans and women, to offer resources they might not otherwise know about.

Start by keeping accurate records for each individual client and be sure to update them on a regular basis. Don't put off writing or typing up your client notes hoping that your memory will hold out until you get around to doing it. There's no better time to do them than directly after a client session when everything is fresh in your mind, even if you only jot basic notes and convert them later to a more formal SOAP or CARE chart. The same goes for updates. Get in the habit of asking a client if there are changes to any of the medical, personal, or lifestyle information on her intake form. Note these changes on an update form as soon as possible. Also stay abreast of changes in a client's contact information, especially cell phone numbers and e-mail addresses as these change frequently. This may seem minor but when it comes to marketing, your best business comes from clients you already have and if you don't know how to reach them, you can't market to them.

How you choose to do your bookkeeping is an individual choice. Choosing between manual record keeping, online and offline software, or obtaining the services of a professional is entirely at your discretion and should be based on which you prefer, what you can afford, and what you feel confident in doing yourself. Because of tax implications it's usually advisable to have an accountant familiar with your business to advise you even if you do most of your financial and tax bookkeeping yourself.

If you decide to forego the idea of hiring a professional, remember that there are many accountants who will barter services with you. You may well be able to exchange work you don't want to do for providing the massage service you love. Regardless of the choice to do it yourself or hire or barter it out, it is imperative that all record keeping is accurate, legible, and accountable. It is your responsibility to make sure you have all the receipts to back up any claims of income and expenses because the burden of proof is on you, not your accountant.

Familiarize yourself with the IRS and SBA website publications regarding home-based businesses. On these sites you will find tax laws, tax forms, worksheets, and videos that help explain everything you need to know about keeping accurate records, recording business transactions, and substantiating certain expense deductions. You will also find programs that may help you to manage your tax obligations at a free or low cost to you.

Whichever avenues of record keeping and tax management you choose for your home-based massage therapy business, take care to do it responsibly. The more concise you are, the more money you'll ultimately keep in your pocket.

09 Professionalism and Ethics

Professionalism means different things to different people. It may be more about your attitude toward your business and the people you work with than a rigidly defined set of dos and don'ts from an industry standard. You display your level of professionalism through integrity, how you communicate, your massage therapy skills, and the business image projection and practices you employ on a daily basis.

Some people mistakenly believe that if they work minimal hours or have a home-based massage business, they can take a more casual approach to professional and ethical practices. In truth, if you have a license to practice massage therapy then this is your profession—not your hobby. Viewing and treating it as such will allow for considerably more success and a much stronger professional image to the public.

A code of ethics goes hand in hand with maintaining a strong degree of professionalism. Integrity and respect are building blocks for a solid ethical practice. You must do what you say you'll do, value your principles and stand by them, and respect yourself and your business, as well as the colleagues and clients you work with each day.

Joining business organizations and associations can help you define professionalism as it pertains to your home-based business and assist you in maintaining a higher standard. Participation in these organizations shows an even greater level of commitment to your chosen field and forms a basis for further business growth from regular interaction with colleagues and other business professionals like yourself.

Some of the more common ethical dilemmas to watch out for in the massage therapy profession are easily rectified, but just as easily missed as an ethical concern. Determine your own code of ethics by following basic industry standards and include others as they pertain to you and your personal and business boundaries. The following are some situations that can arise and may be so minimal that they may be dismissed as insignificant:

- Misrepresenting education, skills, or training
- Sexual impropriety
- Betraying client confidentiality
- Dishonest financial transactions or income reporting
- Working outside the scope of practice
- Misleading advertising or claims

There are certainly other ethical concerns beyond these few. Usually, ethical dilemmas come up when a situation arises that a practitioner just doesn't quite know how to handle. Such is the case when a husband-and-wife team frequents the same massage therapist. Because they share a life at home, it's very common for a spouse to ask questions and express concerns regarding their partner's massage sessions with you. You may know that the other spouse would be perfectly agreeable to you giving out information regarding a session outcome or their particular issue or concerns. Yet if a code of ethics stresses the importance of confidentiality, then you are duty bound to hold that confidence regardless of how well the couple knows one another. The best solution is to state to the inquiring spouse that they will need to

---

Real-Life Story

Beware the modest client as well as the immodest one. I had one client so modest that he wore four pairs of shorts—one over the other—for the first three years he came to me for massage therapy. One day, he came in a single pair and I knew then that trust was firmly established. A European client was asked to disrobe to his comfort level after I left the room and situate himself on the massage table under the sheet and blanket. When I asked if he was ready and re-entered the room, he was standing there leaning against the table completely nude with his arms folded loosely across his chest. With each, I respected the choice to be modest, or not, and draped them appropriately with a sheet for their privacy and mine. Professionalism is your calling card, always.

---

discuss the matter with their spouse. Alternatively, the spouse in question can give written permission for you to discuss the situation or sessions with the other partner. This can get sticky when your clients become long term and you develop a more friendly relationship with them. A wife may be offended if you refuse to give her information regarding her husband. Yet if you stick to your code of ethics from the start, clients will know exactly where you stand and will usually be more understanding and appreciative of your professionalism.

Taking Care of the Client

What does taking care of your client mean to you? Is it simply meeting their goals and desired outcomes for a massage session? If so, this is a great start. Keeping those thoughts in mind when you start each day will help you succeed in getting a loyal client far sooner than any other gimmick or technique that you use. Once that becomes so ingrained in your mind that it is an automatic thought for you each workday, then you can fine-tune the concept of taking care of your client. Tending to the finer details associated with meeting a client's goals and expectations for the session not only helps you retain a regular paying client, but prompts her to talk about you to others, which is the ultimate form of advertising.

Get to Know Your Clientele

Any car salesperson will tell you that it's important to develop a personal relationship with your customer or, in your case, with your client. This means knowing not only her name, but her husband's, children's, and sometimes pet's! Remembering a birthday or thanking a first-time client for her patronage with a handwritten card sets you apart from the practitioner that does not. Knowing (and remembering from session to session) your client's preferences, goal objectives, and having respect for her individual personality traits will go a long way toward developing a good, long-term working relationship.

Noting Preferences

The client record-keeping skills you have developed are effective for use in noting personal preferences a client has for music and the types and scents of lubricants she enjoys. You were, or will be, taught in massage school to remember to ask frequently about personal comfort level and keep in mind that she probably won't tell you unless you ask. The massage therapy room is a vulnerable setting and a client must feel safe and at ease if you wish to retain her business. And though it makes little sense, a client who experiences discomfort on your table, feels too warm or too cold, or is bothered by the amount of pressure you're using, in most instances won't tell you but often will not return to you either. From your practitioner standpoint this seems hardly fair. After all, if we know better we generally do better. You don't want your client to feel uncomfortable and if you knew she was, you'd most likely do whatever you could to rectify the problem. Taking the initiative to ask will keep a good line of communication open between you and your client and, hopefully, eliminate the silent complaints that deter a client from returning. Read my own real-life story above and see how easy it is for even a client who knows to speak up to suffer silently for reasons they simply don't express.

Paying Attention

One activity that will earn you many points with a massage client is to make note of any particular areas where she loves to have a little extra attention. This may be on her scalp, hands, face, or elsewhere. She will feel important when she realizes that you not only heard her, but you offered the extra attention at a future session without her reminding you. Knowing what your client does for work or regular activity is helpful in determining what areas may need focus. Too many practitioners get into the routine of a one-hour, full-body massage and try to effectively parcel out equal time for each body part. without taking into consideration that someone who works as a massage therapist might need you to provide a little extra attention for her hands, which are the tools of her trade, or that a truck driver might need an additional ten minutes on his lower back because he sits all day without good back support.

Effective Listening

Good listening skills are essential to a service-oriented business. Not only must you hear what a client says about the reason he's seeking massage, but you must actively listen to what he wants to share with you about his lifestyle. Oftentimes when you think a client is talking just to make conversation, you will find he shares valuable insights into the mental, spiritual, and physical aspects of his life that reveal why he might be in your office to begin with. This is one of those gray areas, however, and only you can decide when a client is divulging more information than is pertinent to the massage service you are providing, or crossing any of the ethical boundaries you have set.

Take a few minutes to listen when he talks about his day and work frustrations. Realize that sometimes he doesn't feel he has a safe place to say what's on his mind and that it often helps him relax sooner during his massage if he can express what his day was like. Although you aren't a counselor, you truly have an opportunity to make a real difference in a client's life just by the simple act of LISTENING.

The Extra Touch

No matter how profound your technical massage skills, your client wants to feel that she is unique. She does not want to be part of an assembly line of bodies you work on in the course of your day. She has particular needs, expectations, issues, and stressful situations that are hers and hers alone. Therefore, noting her preferences, listening, and getting to know her are really important. But guess what? You can do better than that. You can add more depth to her experience with extra touches that don't have to be costly or difficult. Creativity and a genuine desire to give your client a high-quality experience is all that's required. This has vast appeal to the massage therapist who really wants to add a creative, original flair to her practice, not only to keep it interesting for her client but also for herself. The most important aspect to keep in mind is that your No. 1 priority is meeting the client's goals and needs for each session. But don't overlook the opportunity to exceed her expectations by offering her little "extras" like heated towels or bottled water to create a more memorable and enjoyable session.

On the topic of extras, here is a list of wonderful options to add a special touch to your massage sessions:

- **Warmed towels, socks, and heated table pad.** Because body temperature drops significantly as it relaxes in an unmoving position for a period of time, warmth is a heaven-sent adjunct to a cool weather massage therapy session or for elderly and other clients who are frequently cold in any weather.
- **Bottled water.** As a practitioner, you are taught to encourage a client to drink lots of water after a session to help the body regain balance. Most people will forget before they shut your office door behind them. Having bottled water available to take with them is a good reminder. Add your own business label to the bottle and it doubles as advertising. If you are concerned with the environmental impact of plastic bottles, simply keep a carafe of water and drinking glasses on a table where a client can access them before or after a massage.
- **Special amenities.** For occasions such as birthdays or holidays, offer the element of surprise in the form of a small token of appreciation. It's simply a nice touch for a client to find a note card with a small discount, a wrapped candy, or other seemingly inconsequential item on the massage table to acknowledge her special occasion.
- **Bath robes.** Keep a unisex bathrobe available for a client who may need to get up during a massage to use the rest room.
- **Disposable wipes and hand sanitizer.** Many clients will come directly from work and have the desire to wash hands or feet before a massage session. Although you can avoid contributing to environmental waste by supplying washcloths and towels for this use, you may want to keep disposable wipes and hand sanitizer accessible for quick cleanup.
- **Specific time.** When a client comes to you weekly, he more than likely will appreciate the convenience of scheduling at the same time and on the same day each week. This makes it easier for a client to remember when he is due in and helps cut down on no-show sessions for you.
- **Tips and ideas.** E-mail or share tips specific to a client's needs and interests. E-mailing her lets her know that you don't forget about her when the she leaves your massage office. This is also an ideal way to keep yourself in the mind of those clients who only come in sporadically and may prompt them to schedule another massage session with you.

- **Smile.** Leave your own problems outside your massage office door. When your client enters that space, greet him with a smile. There is no better "extra touch" than that of a genuine smile.

Professional Liability Insurance

Although this could certainly be placed under the next category of "taking care of you," carrying professional, general, and product liability insurance coverage is a good idea to provide for any mishaps or adverse circumstances that may occur while a client is in your place of business. Although a lawsuit is probably unlikely in the massage therapy profession, it's better to protect him, and yourself, in case of such an event. Insurance coverage is offered to massage students at a heavily discounted rate and most schools will require students to carry it in order to attend.

Policies frequently have high limits and cover you no matter where, or however many different places, you work. With some organizations such as ABMP (Associated Bodywork and Massage Professionals) or AMTA (American Massage Therapy Association), insurance coverage is included in the price of the member benefits package.

Many massage insurance providers sweeten the deal by offering free websites, newsletter opt-ins, identity-theft protection, and other benefits. It's a good plan to shop around and research the benefits, limitations, bodywork modalities that are covered, costs, and the ratings of insurance carriers through the major agencies such as Standard and Poor's or A. M. Best. An "A" or higher rating is optimal.

Depending on the type of insurance policies you currently have in effect, specific massage or bodywork liability insurance may be unnecessary. Discuss your professional needs with your current insurance provider to be sure that you have the coverage you need.

Shop carefully and make an informed decision. Do not pay for more than you need, but make sure any insurance products you purchase have your business, and you, fully protected.

Taking Care of You

As stated several times before, massage therapy is demanding physical work. Yet not only is it rigorous for the body, it is also demanding on the mind. Couple this with the aspects of running a business and it becomes imperative to care for your own well-being equally as well as you suggest to your clientele. Some ways to take care of you will be taught in massage therapy school. Ergonomics, or how efficiently you perform your work, will be stressed in every classroom hands-on training situation and for very good reason. Improper body mechanics can cause repetitive strain and other common injuries in the massage profession. These conditions can end an enthusiastic practitioner's career before it really gets underway. In addition, because dealing with the stressors of building a business and providing clients with the best care while hearing their problems day in and day out takes exceptional mental and emotional fortitude, these skills need to be reinforced consistently.

Just as you have a toolbox of massage tools and techniques, so too should you have one prepared with fun, interesting, and inspiring options to use for regular self-care of your own mind, body, and spirit. Keeping your personal balance is fundamental in building a successful career and creating a happy, healthy life.

Nutrition

I'm not an expert on the topic of nutrition. However, as a complementary health-care practitioner, the topic of nutrition often comes to the front. From the viewpoint of self-care, it is universally considered to be a cornerstone of good health.

So what does it mean to me? Nutrition means first and foremost all things in moderation—a simple concept we've all heard a thousand times. Anything can be overdone. Water is essential to life yet if you drink too much of it you probably won't feel very well afterward. And at the same time, an occasional candy bar probably isn't going to shorten your life span either.

Likewise, as mom always said, eat your breakfast. This is another bit of advice that is often quoted. It's repeated because it makes sense. Your body is in rest mode for up to eight hours while you sleep without the intake of fuel to sustain it for the waking part of the day. Just as you wouldn't (or shouldn't) expect your car to move with no gasoline in it, you shouldn't have similar expectations of your body. And no, coffee and a doughnut are not optimal, but you know that. Aim high: Eat a breakfast with fiber and protein so you have the physical and mental fortitude you need to feel great when you meet the first client of the day.

Consider keeping nutrition simple by doing your best to implement a diet that includes plenty of hydration (water) and an assortment of rainbow foods. The rainbow diet consists of eating a multitude of fruits and vegetables in all the colors of the rainbow to add complete nutritional value your body wants and needs to run most efficiently. Then further balance out your nutrition profile with high-quality proteins. If you need help choosing a proper diet for you, consult with your medical practitioner or a nutritionist qualified in assisting you with your own particular needs.

Exercise

Be creative with your exercise regimen in accordance with your doctor's guidelines. Remember that ANY movement is exercise so don't think yard or housework isn't part of your exercise quotient. Any activity that requires motion, strength, and stretching is good exercise, and all activity will help in keeping you agile and strong to be able to provide massage therapy to clients each day. The following are three examples of exercises you may find beneficial in helping you stay strong, healthy, and flexible as a massage practitioner:

1. **Walking.** A hands-down favorite of many is walking. Whether it's a city park, a country road, or around the mall, walking is a good all-purpose activity. It

provides aerobic exercise, strengthens your legs, heart, and lungs and can be a very meditative experience at the same time.

2. **Yoga.** Many massage schools implement a yoga class within the curriculum because of its amazing ability to balance body and mind in the same activity. Strength and agility increases, lung capacity improves, and the body is readily oxygenated through coordinated breathing and poses (asanas). Yoga uses this coordinated breath and movement to discipline the mind to be calm and focused.

3. **Tai chi.** Similar to yoga in principle, tai chi is a gentle, fluid series of movements that coordinate breath work with motion. Tai chi can be incorporated for use with any fitness level.

Mental Fitness

Physical and mental fitness go hand in hand. Each is paramount to a rewarding career in a home-based massage therapy business. It is a wise practitioner who checks in with his mental fitness level on a regular basis to detect stress, burnout, feeling overwhelmed, or other energy-sapping emotions and feelings before they become too difficult to contain. When situations arise that create a "lump in my throat," "knot in the pit of my stomach," or "tight band around my head," it's time to recognize it as a stress response and do something about it.

1. **Meditate.** People often find meditation to be very difficult. The mere thought of sitting in silence is about as excruciating to me as the idea of hearing someone scrape their fingernails on a chalkboard. Yet meditation has the capacity to still mind chatter, reduce stress, and teach us to live in the present moment instead of the past or future by instilling focus.

2. **Guided visualization.** Many people consider guided visualization as equally effective as meditation to help reduce stress levels. It may also be easier to implement because there is a voice to guide you through the relaxation process without the uncomfortable silence of traditional meditation.

3. **Moving meditation.** Qigong, tai chi, yoga, and many other activities qualify as moving meditation. These activities require focus and coordinated breath and movement to gain optimal benefits.

Spiritual Well-Being

Although it can, spiritual well-being does not necessarily mean attending to religious values. Taking care of spirit is inner nourishment—those activities that feed your spirit. This can mean grabbing your camera and shooting photos of your pets, kids, or the sunset. It might constitute going to a sporting event or art show with friends. Feeding your spirit can be as simple as taking time to write in a gratitude journal, take a bubble bath, or get a massage. Or spiritual health, for you, may mean going to church or otherwise connecting to whatever you see as a source greater than yourself. You may not know what it is that feeds your spirit but often you'll recognize it because it rejuvenates you and makes you feel good. As a health-care provider, we spend a good part of our day taking care of others, making it vital that we also take care of our own well-being. Sometimes it's easy to forget to do just that.

Self-Help Techniques

As discussed, many times a massage therapist spends so much time taking care of her clients, family, and friends that she sorely neglects herself. But as you learn more and share what clients can do to help take care of themselves, you will also learn what you can do as a practitioner to take the best care of YOU.

TLC for Your Hands and Body

It can't be stated enough: Your hands are the tools of your trade. It's important to take care of them on a regular basis, so remember not to overlook them even if they don't complain quite as loudly as your shoulders, lower back, or neck.

Paraffin Wax Dipping

Warmed paraffin wax gently coats your hands and imparts a wonderfully soothing effect on the intricate muscles and joints of your fingers and thumbs. If you don't have access to a paraffin wax warmer (I strongly recommend you own one), most full-service salons have them available for use at a reasonable fee. Owning one is the best option, because after a full day's work providing massage there's nothing quite like the relaxing warmth of paraffin to ease stored tensions and ready your hands for the next day's work.

Hand Massage

If you can get someone to massage your hands at the end of the day, wonderful. If you can't (which is likely to be the case), a few simple techniques will help relieve tight muscles and sore finger joints. Use a light oil or lotion and massage one palm with the fingers or thumb of your other hand in slow circular motions. Squeeze in between each knuckle with particular emphasis around the base of your thumbs, which tend to be the workhorse for your hands. Then gently pull, squeeze, and twist each finger in a wringing fashion to relieve pressure located there. Switch hands and then finish by shaking both hands vigorously.

Body Tapping

Body tapping is easy and can invigorate you in minutes. Anyone can do, or be taught, this method to wake up and energize the body. And not only can tapping stimulate, it can also encourage tense, tight muscles to relax and elongate, which makes it a great tool to use on oneself in between client sessions. Apply body tapping by making loose fists. Starting at your head, gently tap all over your head for about thirty seconds. If you want to tap on your face, use your fingertips for even more gentle pressure. Continue more firm, repeated tapping down your neck and across both shoulders. You will need to use one hand and then the other to tap your shoulders. Tap down your forearm, around your hand and up the underside of your arm. Repeat several times then switch to tap the other arm. Use both fists to tap over your chest, then down and around your abdomen. Tap quickly, and firmly but not so hard as to cause pain or discomfort. From the abdominal area tap down the outer and back sides of your legs to your ankles then up the front and inner sides several times. Finally, bend over at the waist and use your fists to tap as much of your back as you can reach giving emphasis to the lower back region. Take a minute to gently shake and twist your body before carrying on with your day.

Aromatherapy

Use essential oils to relax, stimulate, or ease pain. You may already use these pure-plant oils for your clients, but do you use them for yourself? Essential oils must always be used with proper discretion and concern for safety practices. But when used properly, they can be a wonderful adjunct to your self-care routine:

- Add drops of lemon, lime, grapefruit, or tangerine essential oil (or a blend of two or more) to the corners of the stall during your morning shower.

The steam will carry the scent and serve to invigorate you as you start your day.

- Use a few drops of lavender essential oil in oil or lotion to massage your hands at the end of the day. Lavender is renowned for its soothing, relaxing properties and is helpful in preparing one for a good night's sleep.
- Include rosemary and peppermint essential oil in a warm, sea-salt footbath after a long workday to rejuvenate tired feet.

Neck and Shoulder Squeeze

Use the opposite hand to cup and squeeze the back and sides of your neck from the base of your skull to your shoulder. Continue squeezing across your shoulder and down your arm if necessary. Repeat several times before switching sides. The squeezing action helps milk tension and tightness from overused muscles that are sore and tired, and takes only a few minutes to perform whenever needed.

Appearances

You never get a second chance to make a first impression. This often-quoted saying is entirely accurate. What a client first sees of you, your yard, home, and massage space is how he will form his very first impression of your business. It's critical to make sure that first impression is the best one you can put forth because it can easily determine your value in a client's eyes.

How Do I Look?

If you greet me for my first massage session in jeans, sneakers, and a tee shirt from the last concert you went to—regardless of how clean and neat you are, how cheery your smile, or how politely you greet me—my very first thought is *unprofessional*. Like it or not, we form associations in our mind as to what a therapist or health-care practitioner should look like. Seldom do we envision them in a very casual style of dress because we're likely to equate that with lack of quality in a professional setting. Is that unfair? Sure. But again, this section is on appearances and first impressions.

As a massage practitioner you certainly want to be comfortable because you'll be moving around a lot. Yet you can be as comfortable in less casual styles of pants or slacks and functional tops as you can in jeans and tee shirts.

This style of dress is not a hard-and-fast rule. What is important is that you look like the professional you are, not like you just got up from the couch after watching television on a Saturday afternoon. Just as important is to be well-groomed, neat, and clean no matter your attire. This includes keeping long hair pulled back, breath fresh, and nails trimmed. No exceptions.

How Does My Space Look?

Keeping yourself presentable and professional looking is far easier than keeping your home office that way. The home-based business has a distinct disadvantage from the onset because it is in a residential setting versus commercial. This alone lowers its perceived degree of professionalism, so it's in your best interest to be sure to keep the yard, home, and massage space well-maintained and tidy at all times.

It's not always easy to see your environment the way others see it because you're in it daily. It may be helpful to ask a neighbor or friend to give you honest feedback of what they see and feel when they walk into your home environment. Don't take it personally if your friend suggests that the dozen gnome statues lining the walkway, clutter in the entry, or chipped paint on the massage room door might need your attention. Take the feedback in the spirit it was meant and make changes accordingly. Always put forth the extra effort needed to keep your space uncluttered, neutral, and professional looking.

Cleanliness and Sanitation

This is not an option. You must keep yourself and your massage space as clean and sanitary as possible. Most people would not negate the importance of personal hygiene practices like bathing, filing fingernails, teeth brushing, etc. Yet often deep-massage space cleaning and clearing may be done only sporadically and not as well as it could be.

Counter and furniture surfaces should be dust-free, carpets and floors vacuumed daily, and bathrooms sanitized regularly. Options abound for the massage practitioner with a desire to choose organic, environmental, and health-conscious cleaning products. These range from all-purpose cleaners to specific biodegradable bathroom and laundry detergents and cleansers. Many are irritant-free, which is appreciated by the client with allergies to certain chemicals or scents.

Regardless of what cleaning agents you decide are best for your practice, the best suggestion is to put them to use as often as you would in any other health-care profession. The well-being of your client is always of utmost importance.

Policies

The policies you implement for your home-based massage therapy business are the "road rules" for your practice. These policies constitute what you expect from a client as well as letting them know what they can expect from you. All policies should be in writing, posted in your massage space, and a copy given to all clients. Remember to evaluate and make changes to any outdated policies and procedures at least once a year.

Some standard policy topics to consider are listed below. Depending on your situation, this may not be an exhaustive list.

- **Late or missed appointment fees:** Will you charge a fee when a client misses an appointment? Will you provide them a full sixty minutes from the time they arrive if they show up late? Keep in mind the bottom line: Time is money.
- **Cancellations:** Will you allow a client to call ten minutes before a scheduled appointment and cancel? Or will you require a twenty-four-hour cancellation notice?
- **Communicable diseases:** How will you handle the issues of communicable diseases? Most common will be the client who arrives with the common cold or flu symptoms. How will you communicate that massage may make them feel worse as well as expose you?
- **Sexual misconduct:** How will you verbalize that inappropriate sexual language and actions will not be tolerated?
- **Privacy:** Clients, especially those new to bodywork, really appreciate assurance that their privacy in your space with you is guaranteed.
- **Confidentiality:** As with privacy, clients want, and deserve, a commitment to confidentiality.

Professional Conduct

Professional conduct on the part of you, the massage practitioner, encompasses everything from how you answer your phone to the massage skills you use with your clients. Courtesy, professional knowledge, business sense, public relations, and many other attributes make up the code of conduct that you must employ each and every day to run an effective and successful business. Without them, you're sunk.

As a licensed massage therapist, my typical workday looks like this:

I get ready for work and arrive no less than thirty minutes before my first client is due. This assures that I prepare the space accordingly, putting on fresh linens, table warmer if needed, and setting out drinking water and other potential necessities. I look over the client's recent updated SOAP note to refresh myself on his needs and the work we've done previously to address those.

I take a few minutes to make sure I drink some water (always have breakfast to maintain energy levels during the session) and clear my mind of any and all thoughts that may distract from my client's session. My mantra is, and has always been, to leave my problems outside my office door and make the time I spend with my client, his.

When my client arrives, I greet him with a smile and courteous small talk. This conversation is directed so that it expresses an interest in what's happening with him (i.e., "How are you today?") yet is not so lengthy or in depth as to deter me from my scheduled day. These few minutes are also the time where I will discover what his bodywork needs are today.

The client is left in privacy to prepare for his session. I knock and wait for a response before I enter the room to be sure he is ready. The massage session ensues and I stay in tune to any verbal or nonverbal communications (i.e., "that hurts," body language, tensing muscles) to assure his comfort level and that we are addressing his concerns.

After the session ends, I let him know that I will leave the room again, assuring his privacy to regain full alertness and get dressed again. (Some clients—elderly, ill, pregnant, and others—may require my assistance and therefore, for their safety, I do not leave the room in these instances.)

When he is ready we take a few minutes to discuss any improvements, suggestions, or concerns that he has. I offer to set his next massage session, collect my fee, and say a friendly goodbye. I take the opportunity before the next client's arrival to record his payment and update his notes to reflect the work we did in the session with any instructions I want to remember for his next appointment.

I clean up immediately after each person, replacing sheets and sanitizing the table and equipment used. At the end of the workday, I always clean my workspace completely so it is fresh and ready for the next day's setup.

Laundry is the next priority in my day. Sheets and towels cannot be left for long periods of time without washing due to the lubricants used. Many oils turn rancid and break down the linen fibers, resulting in the need to throw them out sooner than if they are washed as quickly as possible. Using special grease-cutting detergents and non-staining lubricants will reduce this problem.

After the last client is gone and cleanup is finished, it's time to return phone calls and set upcoming appointments. Regardless of the difficulty or ease of my day, I put on a smile as I speak so the client hears it in my voice.

Note that with a home-based business, unless you have a separate business phone line, it can sometimes be hard to draw the line that officially ends your workday phone calls. Only you can determine if you will use voice mail, a service, or some other way to reduce client calls in the evening hours that would otherwise be dedicated to family or personal time.

Time Management

It is said that if you don't manage your time, time will manage you. Never is this truer than in a home-based business where the atmosphere is generally more relaxed than in a more formal workplace. Maintaining a firm commitment to effective time-management strategies is a crucial factor in preventing the business from failing.

If we take a good look at how we plan and implement the events of our day, it may be a shock to find how many hours are wasted in nonproductive activity. Watching television, reading, answering e-mail, chatting with family or friends on the phone, and texting are all notorious time wasters that most of us are guilty of overdoing.

Unlike the traditional work environment, the home-based practitioner has the unique situation of balancing work and home life in the same setting. This is no small feat. As has been mentioned previously, sometimes the line between personal life and work life becomes obscured. Because of this, time management becomes even more vital to maintain order in both your personal life and your business.

Using some sort of monitoring system to track your daily activity is more effective than trying to store it all in your head. A cell phone, PDA, computer program, or even a calendar or day planner are all useful to record what needs to be done. Make a concerted effort to plan out your day in advance by scheduling the night before. This helps to not only think clearly about what needs to be done the next day, but also gets it off your mind in preparation for a good night's sleep.

Do you find yourself doing any of the following?

- Procrastinating
- Not prioritizing tasks according to degree of importance
- Doing several things at once
- Taking on projects too large for you to handle alone
- Running on empty or not resting
- Allowing distractions to interfere with priority tasks

Make a to-do list the night before and follow it the next day. Save your high-priority projects (such as marketing) or those that require a large degree of concentration for the parts of your day where you personally experience peak energy. As a massage therapist, you will have to be creative and weave the tasks of your day in between client sessions. Do this by taking care of yourself, taking breaks, eating well, and practicing stress-relief activities. Discipline yourself to tackle your to-do list immediately and don't allow distractions like e-mail or text messages keep you from completing the tasks you've set for your day.

Dilemmas: What to Say and Do

A discussion on dilemmas is something you may not encounter in other books or in massage therapy class. In this section particular, yet common, dilemmas are noted that you may, or may not, come across in your tenure as a licensed massage therapist. Massage practitioners are frequently asked questions, such as "What do you do when . . . ?" "What do you do if . . . ?" and "How do you deal with . . . ?" Trial and error is the typical way to learn how to deal with these questions and others. Here you'll get some of the answers.

(Please note: The following scenarios have been part of my professional life as well as other massage therapists I have known. How I handle them is not the only ways they can be dealt with, but they are ways that have been most useful for me without creating undue stress or embarrassment to me or the client. It is also worth mentioning that the sexual situations I reference are from a female-practitioner-to-male-client perspective. That's because I AM a female practitioner. The scenario could just as easily be reversed to reflect the relationship of the male practitioner with a female client or a same-sex practitioner and client and in no way is meant to show bias.)

"What do you do when someone hints at or asks you for sex when they call for an appointment?"

Pre-screen your clients when they call before you ever see them in your office. Most private-practice massage therapists operate on a "by appointment only" basis so screening is much simpler. While you have potential clients on the phone, ask questions and listen to cues. Potential problem clients may frequently want immediate appointments and will say they are "just passing through the area." Some males will be straightforward and ask if you provide "happy endings," which is release of sexual tension by means of ejaculation. Others will be less upfront and may ask only what kind of massage you do, yet they may be unwilling or hesitant to disclose their full name or phone number to you when setting a massage appointment. If you have caller ID, you may see the phone numbers listed as private. This can mean they have their numbers blocked or may be calling from a public place such as a pay phone. Certainly this may mean nothing at all, but erring on the safe side is prudent. If your intuition tells you that callers may be looking for more than non-sexual massage, better to know in the pre-screening call so you can make it understood politely and professionally that you only provide therapeutic massage.

"How do you deal with a guy who gets an erection during massage?"

This is actually a common experience. It doesn't necessarily mean that the man is having improper sexual thoughts toward you (though it can). An erection is a normal

---

Real-Life Story

Learning to screen new potential clients over the phone is a valuable skill. Inevitably, the call will come that asks for sexual services. One of the first calls I ever took was when a male caller asked if I did "release." "Of course!" I unhesitatingly replied. After all, release of muscle tension is what I specialized in! With further discussion, I realized that the form of release he was referring to was that of a sexual nature. Fortunately, we were on the phone and he couldn't see my embarrassment. I regained my composure and professionally (and respectfully) explained that I misunderstood, my massage service was therapeutic only, and that I didn't offer what he was asking for.

response triggered by relaxation of the nervous system and an increase in overall circulation. First and foremost, don't panic. Know that it's normal. Keep your client draped properly with a sheet or blanket and keep it loose around his midsection in the event that he does have a spontaneous erection. An erection is not something you as a practitioner need to verbally address unless it's in addition to sexual comments made by the client. If sexually oriented actions or conversations begin, stop the session immediately and inform the client politely that the massage is for therapeutic purposes only. If the behavior continues let him know that you will need to end the massage session if the actions persist and he will be responsible for payment for the full appointment time.

"What do you do if a client asks you out?"

This is an issue of ethics. If you have made a list of your values, you may have already decided not to mix your business and personal lives. In smaller communities where everyone knows everyone, this may be harder to do. If this situation does arise, determine if you want to see the client on a social level. If so, simply terminate the client-practitioner relationship if it conflicts with your policies, values, and beliefs, or state and local laws.

"How do you handle people that come in that are heavyset, have warts, moles, excessive hair, or other stuff?"

Treat her with absolute respect, kindness, and a smile. People are very self-conscious of their bodies. When she comes to a therapist for a massage session, she will frequently be completely undressed on the massage table and feel exposed and vulnerable even though she is covered. Let her know that your massage office is a safe space for her to relax and receive nonjudgmental therapeutic bodywork. Reassure her that she will be allowed complete privacy before and after her session to prepare and that she will be draped with a sheet or blanket at all times during her massage. Listen for verbal cues of insecurity or doubt and address it in a kind, professional manner that conveys trust.

"What do you do if a client smells of body odor or strong perfume?"

In your pre-screening, initial phone call, let the potential client know how to prepare for her session (even if she says she's had massage before) by showering, removing all jewelry, and refraining from wearing any scents beyond that of deodorant. For those clients who may arrive directly from work or other activities, some massage practitioners have a shower available for the client to use pre-massage. If this isn't an option, disposable wipes or wash cloths, and hand towels should be readily accessible.

"How do you handle a client that makes an appointment and then doesn't show up or shows up late?"

Many, but not all, massage therapists have a set policy of charging a percentage or the full fee for a missed appointment. To stay on the daily schedule, the therapist may give only the remaining appointment time available when a client arrives late. Making sure to notify clients in advance of these policies, if in effect, is important to maintain good client-practitioner relation where both parties know what is expected.

"My husband came to see you last week. I asked how his appointment was and all he said was 'good.' How do YOU think he is?"

As stated before, a policy of client confidentiality should be firmly implemented from the very first day you open the doors to your business. Let her know you cannot disclose any information about her partner's massage therapy session but that you can give her a consent form to have him sign giving you permission to talk with her about his session.

"Your massage is $65 an hour. Can you give me a better price?"

Your massage office is not a car dealership or an outdoor market where negotiating prices is the norm. You set your massage therapy rates based on what similar professionals are charging in your area, your budget, and goals you've set. You may, or may not, have multisession or senior-citizen discounts available. No matter your rates, discounts, sales, or specials, YOU must be in control of those prices—not the client. Once you let a client "talk you down," you'll lose the ability to maintain a consistent income because he will expect if you made concessions once or twice that you will every time. He may spread the word as well that you can be haggled with, and that may become an even bigger problem with being paid your regular hourly rate.

(*Author's note: In discussing this issue with other professionals, there have been some who disagree with my opinion as stated above. Some believe that a practitioner will possibly lose prospective clients by not negotiating. I say maybe so, yet if you are marketing regularly, you can replace the clients who want to pay less than the going rate with those that will. Because I believe in working smarter, not harder, I would prefer* *to see five clients paying the full $65 rate than the seven it would take to make nearly the same money paying $50 an hour. Never reduce your worth.)*

"What do you do if you mis-schedule a client?"

If you're in business long enough, there will come a time when you will schedule a client for 2 p.m. but think it was 3 p.m. and show up late. (This is not so much of an issue with a home office.) Or an emergency may arise and you may totally forget to notify a client that you can't provide his scheduled massage. It's important to remember that MISTAKES HAPPEN. Let your client know you acknowledge the value of his time, apologize sincerely, and offer a free or deeply discounted session. He will most often appreciate your sincerity and offer. Do your best not to let being late or missing your client appointments become your habit. If you do, you will gain a reputation for unreliability and your client will find someone he CAN count on.

"But I'm a guy. I don't want to have another guy give me a massage! (Or alternatively, I'm a woman. I would be uncomfortable having a man give me a massage.)"

Male massage therapists statistically have more difficulty excelling in the massage profession than a female. In large part this is because traditionally a sexual connotation has followed the massage profession even though its reputation as a viable health-and-wellness modality continues to increase annually. The fact remains that male practitioners receive the same massage training as females and can have identical skills, empathy, caring, compassion, and desire to help others as any of their female colleagues. It rests heavily on women in the profession to educate the public so males have equal opportunity for success as licensed massage therapists.

"So, you work in a massage parlor?"

Respond in a pleasant voice (smile as you talk to help with this), "I have a great massage studio here in town. Have you ever had a massage before?" You have effectively replaced the word "parlor" with "studio" without sounding chastising AND you are opening the door to a potential new client by opening the conversation with a question.

"Can I get a rub (or rubdown)?"

Again, in a pleasant voice say something like, "I provide massage therapy for general wellness or for many different types of physical complaints. How can I help you?"

"Are you the masseuse?"

Response: "I'm the massage therapist, yes. How can I help you?" Remember to smile as you talk whether it's face to face or on the phone.

"Do you do happy endings?"

Stay professional and composed. This is hard to do the first few times you are asked this question. Simply reply, "No. I provide therapeutic massage only." At this point, you may get a polite response of "thank you" or "goodbye" or simply hear the click as the caller hangs up. It's OK either way. You handled the conversation exactly as you should.

These are a few commonly asked questions or dilemmas in the massage industry and all practitioners will face them at one point or other. What do you do when they arise? Keep your answers professional without being stuffy. Remember that your purpose is to educate about massage benefits and provide therapeutic bodywork. Part of that educational process is demolishing the ancient image of the backroom massage parlor where more than a rubdown commonly took place. Are some of those facilities still in operation today? Of course, but if you are a licensed practitioner who only offers therapeutic massage, then it is part of your professional responsibility to share the proper terminology for your massage office or studio and the information that you provide therapeutic massage (versus a rub or rubdown and happy endings). The word *masseuse* is basically harmless and most people recognize it readily. Yet the controversy remains over whether it is connected in people's minds with the massage parlor and the image of happy endings or the massage office and the therapist who is trained in the scientific manipulation of the soft tissues of the body for therapeutic purposes. Just as you use your hands for skillful massage work, use your word skills to convey the proper terms to others.

What Does Professionalism Look Like to You?

Though "professionalism, professionalism, professionalism" should be your mantra, it's too vague. Professionalism has different meaning for everyone and is conveyed according to their own beliefs, values, and ideas. When embarking on a massage therapy career, home-based or not, really take time to consider what professionalism means to you.

Determine how best to take care of your clientele to keep people coming back. You want a client to remember you and return when she needs massage or other bodywork that you offer. Make her feel special each visit by listening, remembering things she's told you about her family or personal issues, providing bodywork techniques and add-on services to address her individual needs, and expressing a genuine interest and caring every time she walks through your door.

Take care of you. Sometimes it's easy to focus all your energy as a massage practitioner on what you can do for your client. When you don't keep a healthy balance between taking care of you and taking care of your clientele, you wake up one day burned out with emotional and physical exhaustion. So eat well, exercise (beyond the bodywork you do daily), and take care of your own mental and spiritual needs each day. Remember that you can't do your best if you don't feel your best.

Carry adequate amounts of liability insurance in the rare occurrence that a client slips, has an adverse reaction to massage lotion, or some other situation arises that may incite a lawsuit. After being out of school and in the profession for some time you may feel that you are throwing money out the window each year by paying for insurance coverage you've never needed. But by not carrying it, you must assume full risk if something should happen. Only you can decide if it's worth it.

Examine your values, beliefs, and the code of conduct recommended by any professional massage organization you are a member of to assist in determining your own business policies and procedures. These will provide the road map for how you conduct your business. Professionalism and ethics will help you determine your boundaries and lay the groundwork for effectively managing dilemmas that will undoubtedly arise.

Finally, manage your time well. How you begin your day determines how productive your day will be, so start out strong with a good game plan in mind for the day's schedule. Be disciplined in the management of your time so that time doesn't manage you.

Let the World Know You Are Here! The Marketing Piece

The bottom line: If people don't know you're in business, they won't come to you. This seems like an obvious statement but many new practitioners seem to think that setting up shop and getting a listing in the phone directory is all that's necessary to starting a massage therapy business. Rest assured that if this is the approach you choose, you have failed before you begin. Not only do you need to adequately promote yourself in the beginning stages of your practice, you must also regularly and methodically market yourself each and every week. Consistency is the key and marketing doesn't always require a lot of money. Be creative, use some of the ideas presented, come up with some of your own, and get down to business.

Practice Talking about What You Do

As suggested in an earlier chapter, when someone asks what you do and you respond with "I'm a massage therapist," you will likely get a response of a nod or "Oh." On occasion the person will ask further questions but often you have that one chance to educate and potentially interest the person in coming to you for massage.

Talking about what you do is sometimes called an elevator speech. It basically means telling what you do in the time it would take to ride in an elevator up a few floors. The components of the elevator speech consist of what you do, who you do it for, and how it benefits them. It should be clear, concise, short, and memorable. After that, if it generates more questions from the person you're speaking to, even better because it shows you've piqued their interest.

The benefits should be that which entices a perspective client to learn more about you and what you offer. This is commonly referred to as a USP or unique selling proposition. Without a USP to make you stand out, you're just one more fish in a very big pond.

Once you've honed your elevator speech, practice it over and over until it comes across naturally and easily. Breathe, smile, and keep your shoulders lowered. Practic-ing in front of a mirror and then later recording your speech will help you to perfect it until it becomes second nature and you can say it readily in any circumstance.

Choose Your Target Market

You are a salesperson. "No," you say, "I'm a massage therapist!" Welcome to the world of owning your own business. Working for one's self means having several job descriptions, one of which is being a salesperson. If you can't sell yourself and your services, you have no business.

So as a salesperson, you learn how to give an elevator speech. The more you give this speech, the more YOU will know what you do. The more you know what you do, the better you can choose your target market or markets to aim for.

Many therapists make the common mistake of not creating a brand or niche for themselves. This goes back to an earlier topic on being the massage practitioner who attempts to provide for the needs of everyone. "Jack of all trades, master of none" is a common saying to describe this type of therapist.

Think of it like this: You want to shoot an arrow at a spot on the side of a barn. Do you have a better chance of hitting your target by simply shooting your arrow at the barn or by painting a red bull's-eye there and aiming your bow and arrow at that?

When you cast your marketing arrows in no particular direction, you probably won't reach the targeted clientele that would be most receptive to the services you state in your elevator speech. Searching for the target market you want not only gives laser focus to the audience most interested in using your services and products, but also cuts down the costs of blanket marketing to the people who won't.

As an example of niche, or target, marketing, say you want to specialize in pre-natal and infant massage. Where will you look for clients? Does it make sense to post your literature at the local gym just because women go there as well as men? Maybe, but is it the most focused option for bringing you droves of prospective clients? Probably not.

On the other hand, because pregnant women and those with babies frequent the local obstetrician's and pediatrician's offices, these are good starting points. Contact the offices and ask if you can place literature there. Ask if you can include educational massage therapy material (with your business info added) to the office welcome packet usually provided to new patients. Learn your elevator speech so that you can deliver it in person. Remember to make it good because often you only have one chance to make a great impression. Once you have your materials in place, continue to keep good rapport with the office staff. Offer some sort of thank you occasionally: a floral arrangement, fruit basket, or even a free massage for the office manager or whomever approved placement of your literature.

Other areas in which to promote your pre-natal or infant massage practice are wellness or baby fairs, birthing classes, stores that specialize in maternity and infant needs, or schools that may have a community bulletin board to post contact information.

You may not want to limit your business to one market like pre-natal and infant massage therapy. Regardless if you choose one niche or three, be sure to connect with the people most likely to use your services to get the biggest bang for your marketing buck.

Your Image

As previously suggested, what you decide to use for a massage therapy logo depends largely on the type of image you wish to portray to potential clientele. Typically, massage logos for signage, websites, clothing, letterhead, brochures, and business cards are soothing and convey a sense of relaxation and comfort. On the other hand, a massage practitioner who provides mainly medical massage may want to design a logo that denotes a more clinical (yet still soothing) look versus one that is more flowery or Zen-like. For any logo design here are some basic elements:

- **Essentials.** Your business name, your name, location, and contact information are important.
- **Imagery.** Healing hands, massage therapy images, or nature photographs are all applicable in conveying a message of relaxation or healing.
- **Specialty.** Determine what makes you stand out from others. Once you decide, break it down into a few words, for example, "specializing in deep relaxation."
- **Clarity.** Choose your font carefully. Many script fonts are flowing and beautiful, but not easily readable to the casual viewer, especially on small pieces such as business cards. Stick with fonts like Verdana or Times New Roman to catch and hold the reader's eye.
- **Colors.** Softer, muted colors are commonly used in massage therapy logos because of how color affects a person's emotions. Softer colors are associated with a sense of calm.

Oftentimes your business image is presented to someone through your website, written literature, and the information they contain before she or he ever meets you. Because of this, it's so important that the image you project is one that distinctly conveys professionalism, caring, and healing, whether it's from a spa or relaxation-based perspective or a clinical one.

Essentials

Although there are probably hundreds or thousands of marketing techniques to employ, there are a select few that would be considered basics to most businesses. Some primary promotional methods include the tried-and-true, such as listing in the phone book yellow pages, handing out business cards, public speaking, or participating in wellness fairs. Giving out personalized items such as pens or stress balls with your business name and contact information imprinted on them is another commonly used marketing strategy, as is holding a business open house or informational presentation.

No matter the promotional method, the premise behind it is always to gain the attention and interest of current and prospective clients. How you do that depends on how you can differentiate your business from a similar practitioner's. Some of the factors in determining your unique advantage include the convenience of the location of your practice, the business image you wish to project, client treatment results, and the range of services you provide. The more you have to offer in benefits to your clients, the more you will set yourself apart from the rest. Marketing these benefits to the people who are enthusiastic about, and will use, the services you offer and who will then tell others about you is exactly how to best use your time and efforts.

So once you've decided how your practice is different from someone else's and you've got your business listed in the yellow pages, what else can you do to promote and get your name in front of more people?

Sample Business Card

BUSINESS NAME

There's more to life than increasing its speed.
~ Gandhi

PRACTITIONER NAME

000 MAIN STREET
ANYTOWN, ANYSTATE 00000
(000) 000-0000
E-MAIL ADDRESS • WEBSITE

For starters, know what marketing consists of. Marketing is selling yourself and your services. Effective marketing consists of knowing what benefits you offer to your clients (not just the services, but how those services can help them), public relations within your locale (educating the public about who you are and what you do), and, through advertising, consistently putting yourself and your business in front of the people who will use your massage therapy services.

The practitioner of a home-based massage therapy business may be under the impression that she can slack off on marketing efforts because she doesn't have the overhead of an outside office location. The fact remains that you have begun this journey as a massage therapist to 1) help people by educating and providing hands-on therapy, and 2) earn an income. Without regular and effective marketing efforts, you won't get the traffic to provide either.

Secondary Promotional Techniques

There are many, many ways to promote your business. There are the basics as listed above (some of which are expanded on the following list), but other options abound and new ones are created daily. You're limited only by your imagination and best of all, many of the best ones are not expensive to implement.

- **Signage.** If you are in an area that allows it, put up a quality, highly visible sign with your business name and phone number on it. It's a one-time investment, other than maintenance, that speaks for itself without you needing to do anything more than put it up.

- **Phone directory listings.** Although fast becoming antiquated, using the phone book yellow pages is still a standard way to advertise. Online phone directories are also an option with more people using the Internet to find what they want.

- **JV marketing.** Joint-venture marketing in massage therapy is cross-promoting with other area businesses. You promote Sarah's hair salon in your massage therapy practice and she promotes your massage business to her clientele. This way you reach far more people than either of you can do on your own.

- **Word of mouth.** Perhaps still the best form of advertising, word of mouth is the referral of your business from a client to other people. This is why it's vitally important to have satisfied clients. If they are thrilled with you and the benefits they receive in your massage practice, they will inevitably tell someone else who may also decide to come to you. Offering an incentive like discounted massage time as a thank-you for giving referrals can be beneficial.

- **Literature posting.** Placement of brochures and business cards in other businesses who may have a bulletin board for such things may land you a client or two. Again, other than the initial time it takes to put up literature, there isn't much else to do other than check from time to time to place more. Use your time most strategically by placing such materials in complementary business establishments such as hair salons, natural food stores, doctor's or chiropractor's offices, and the like.

- **Charitable donations.** Give massage gift-card donations to auctions and other fund-raisers to raise awareness of your business. Don't give more than you can afford even though it may be tax deductible.

- **Wellness events.** Although these are usually free service events, they are an ideal way to educate and get your name and contact information out to people. The added bonus is potential clients can meet you and experience massage firsthand, which may lead them to booking an appointment with you.

- **Newsletters.** Send out a monthly or quarterly regular-mail or e-mail newsletter to current clients to educate them and keep you in the forefront of their minds. Update them on specials or changes in your rates and include an educational topic such as stress relief that they might find useful.

BUSINESS NAME

*There's more
to life
than increasing
its speed.*

~ Gandhi

PRACTITIONER NAME

000 MAIN STREET, ANYTOWN
ANYSTATE 00000 • (000) 000-0000
E-MAIL ADDRESS • WEBSITE

How can you benefit from massage?

Massage and bodywork releases chronic tension and pain, allowing the body to effectively relax and rejuvenate. It can improve circulation, increase joint mobility, reduce blood pressure, and relieve mental and physical stress and anxiety. Massage is known for its ability to improve posture, promote faster healing of injured tissue, improve sleep quality and concentrative ability, and facilitate an overall greater sense of well-being.

What types of massage and bodywork are there?

To date, there are hundreds of variations of massage, bodywork, and somatic therapy modalities.

The following are some of the techniques combined in our practice to give each client a truly individualized session:

Swedish Massage:
The most common form used mainly to relax muscles and ease aches and pains.

Acupressure:
Application of finger pressure along points of the acupuncture meridians, or pathways, used to reduce blockages in these energy pathways to facilitate well-being.

Reflexology:
Massage of the hands, feet, or ears to stimulate points that correspond to areas of the body.

Reiki:
An Eastern technique used to assess imbalances in the energetic field of the body and affect it in such a way as to bring about balance within the body.

Aroma-Stone:
The combination of aromatherapy and hot (and sometimes cold) stone massage. Designed for optimal relaxation through the use of penetrating warmth.

Aromatherapy:
The use of therapeutic-grade essential oils blended with pure base oils to induce relaxation and treat a variety of common complaints.

*Call today to schedule
your integrated massage and bodywork session.*

You'll be glad you did!

- **Social networks.** Facebook, LinkedIn, Twitter, and other social networking sites all have a viable place in keeping your business front and center. These give you the option to stay connected with potential clients, current clients, and other professionals. See chapter 11 for more details.
- **Magnet marketing.** Statistically the common magnet stays on a refrigerator seven years. A business card handed out probably won't make it from the car. Business-card magnets are a way to keep your contact information at a person's fingertips and in clear view.
- **Newspaper columns.** Some smaller newspapers take submissions from community members on different topics. Getting a regular writing gig on the massage profession promotes you as an expert in your field.
- **Community calendar listings.** For a one-time fee, advertising on a community calendar promotes your business for an entire year and can be seen in hundreds to thousands of homes.
- **Direct mail.** Practitioners use this route to send out mass mailings via the postal service (usually in card format enclosed in the newspaper). A questionable option for massage therapists, these mailings may be thrown away before being looked at and, because of broad circulation, may not target the specific clientele you are looking to reach.
- **Networking groups.** Joining professional massage therapy organizations and local business networking groups allows you to make contacts that establish trust and promote your business.
- **Online professional trade directories.** Promoting yourself through massage directories assures that you are targeting those clients that are looking for your services.
- **Public education.** Do you specialize? If geriatric massage is an area that you have more experience or additional training in, perhaps you could use that knowledge to educate at senior centers or target groups of people who are learning how to take care of aging parents.
- **Premiums.** Print your business logo and contact information on various products. Premiums are best used to hand out at local wellness fairs or expos to draw attention to your business. Consider printing on stress balls, pens, handheld self-massage tools, and bags. Though the business card magnet is by far the most useful (and most widely kept) tool in product printing choices, there are many other items that are easy to print your business information on.

These items can be fun, useful gifts to give to clients and prospective clients, but may not be conducive to a small budget.

■ **Pick up the phone.** The best way to get a client is to keep him to begin with. Use e-mail or a phone call to contact a client you haven't seen for a while, let him know you have some available times and ask if he'd like to schedule one of them. The worst he'll say is no. Most of the time a client will be grateful you thought of him even if he can't make an appointment at that time.

■ **Set up an open house.** You can hold an open house in your home office or, alternatively, use a joint venture with another complementary business such as a hair salon. Ask if a local salon, yoga studio, or health-food store is having an open house and if you can participate. Free massage (five to ten minutes per person) is always welcome to patrons and it's an attractor for the business holding the open house. Introduce yourself.

■ **Teach a class.** Teach a stress-relief class for adult education in your community. Present several ways people can reduce stress with a primary focus on the benefits of massage therapy.

Examples of Networking Groups

Chamber of commerce: Chambers work on different levels from local to national. Local chamber of commerce groups help create business-to-business networking connections, offer educational opportunities, and provide support for area business owners.

Leads groups: Leads groups facilitate the introduction of businesses to potential new customers and clients for their products and services.

BNI: Similar to leads groups, BNI is a widespread business networking organization that is broken down into local chapters where business owners meet potential new customers or gain leads and business referrals.

Massage Therapy on LinkedIn: A free-to-join social networking site used mainly to make and maintain business contacts. The massage therapy group is for therapists to support and educate one another in their profession.

Client Retention

Any long-term massage therapist will tell you that it's far easier to keep an existing client than find a new one, which makes this section well worth giving more than just a quick skim. To put this concept in perspective, you must figure what is called the lifetime value of a client. A client's lifetime value is determined by the frequency of visits and the average amount of money she spends with you over a period of time. This value is easier to determine over a period of six months or longer. Here's an example: If Mary comes in once a week at $55 per visit for a period of five years, her "value" is calculated by multiplying $55 by fifty-two weeks, which equals $2,860. Multiply $2,860 by five years and your client's value is now $14,300.

Now consider that same client's value if she purchases products or add-on services. Keep in mind she has been seeing you for massage for five years and you have an established professional relationship with her. She trusts you and is far more likely to purchase products you recommend or utilize additional services you offer. Depending on the type and values of these products and services, you can effectively increase her lifetime value beyond the standard massage therapy she already uses.

Many people who come for massage will be a "once and done" client for various reasons but it makes sense to follow up with some basic efforts to try to retain them as regulars if at all possible.

How do you do that? Build rapport. Rapport is a trusting and professional connection with a new or existing client. Active listening, making eye contact, smiling, educating, and providing positive therapy results are the foundation of building rapport.

Beyond the basics, the following will have a positive impact on developing a long-term relationship with a client:

- **Acknowledge personal information a client shares about family, work, etc.** She knows you work with many clients and will often be surprised and pleased that you remembered things she told you.
- **Give an extra ten minutes of massage every so often.** Let her know it's because you value her patronage. Always check beforehand to make sure her schedule will allow it.
- **Make a follow-up phone call after a session**. This may not be something you want to do with every client each visit, but should always be done after an initial session or after particularly in-depth massage work.

- **Send a thank-you note to a new client expressing your appreciation that he chose you to provide massage for him.** Thank him for his patronage and warmly welcome him to re-book a session at his convenience or contact you should he have any questions or concerns.
- **Ask a new client (or existing one) to book another appointment while you have her in your office.** If she's new to your practice and depending on why she came in to begin with, this is an optimal time to educate her on the cumulative effects of massage. Many existing clients will appreciate scheduling ahead and feel great from the massage they just had and are more likely to re-book on the spot. Some practitioners are timid about asking for a booking. In reality, the very most that can happen is a client will say no. It's OK if she doesn't, but if she does you've got another session on the books.
- **Send birthday cards.** Most people love to be remembered on their special day. They will appreciate that you thought of them. An added bonus is to offer a birthday discount with an expiration date to entice them to re-book.
- **Be professional.** Be warm, courteous, empathetic, sympathetic, and kind at all times. Don't talk about your problems. The client must be assured that the session time is for her and about her. You must convey that the first time

Sample Birthday Card

Happy Birthday!

BUSINESS NAME
PRACTITIONER NAME
000 MAIN STREET, ANYTOWN, ANYSTATE 00000 • (000) 000-0000
E-MAIL ADDRESS • WEBSITE

you give a massage and every time thereafter to gain, and keep, her trust and loyalty.

- **Find out what his needs are.** Ask questions, listen well, and follow through on meeting a client's needs on a consistent basis. Meeting a client's specific needs will go much further than anything else you use to garner business or loyalty.
- **Give regulars their own time slot.** If Carol books weekly, biweekly, or monthly, give her the same time and day each session. Knowing she's scheduled every Monday at 2 p.m. not only helps with her weekly scheduling, but also lets her know you value her business enough to set this time for her and nobody else.

The Marketing Plan

As with any other facets of your home-based massage therapy business, you must have a viable plan for marketing your business in order to not waste money, time, and effort on ineffective methods to attain clients. Using the ideas listed above is good, but there must be consistency and order in the way they are used for optimal efficiency. Marketing is not simply advertising your massage services. It's a repeated effort at putting you and your business in front of the people who will use your services, and requires a more methodical approach than hanging your shingle and listing in the yellow pages.

The following marketing sample questions give an idea of how to strategically plan your marketing efforts to your best advantage:

1. What massage modalities do you specialize in or where do your interests lie? You may have multiple areas and that's OK. You simply need to know what they are so you can aim your marketing arrows at the right targets.
2. Who is the market you want to focus on that would be interested in the services and products you provide? Where will you find these potential clients? As discussed earlier, a massage therapist specializing in pre-natal massage would have more success marketing in an obstetrician's office than in the local gym even though women abound in both locations.
3. What techniques will you employ to initiate contact with these groups and educate them on the massage therapy services you provide? Repeatedly putting your name in front of people is an essential component to good marketing.
4. How will you retain these people as clients once you have them? What benefits will they receive if they continue to see you for massage?

The Marketing Schedule

The keys to effective marketing are efficient time management, consistent application of marketing methods, and periodic assessment of the results achieved. A massage practitioner wants to devote the majority of her time to the healing art she is trained in. Yet marketing is a necessity that can't be overlooked, and a few to several hours a week should be devoted to the practice in order to build and maintain a successful massage business.

How Will You Allow Marketing to Work for You?

Your elevator speech, that thirty-second spiel that is going to depict clearly and concisely who you are, what you do, and the benefits someone will receive by seeing you for massage is a major player in forming a successful massage therapy practice. Working from a home-based office makes it slightly more difficult to practice your speech out in the general public, but you'll do yourself a big favor if you make the effort during your downtime during the week, at night, and on weekends. First and foremost, you have to sell YOU before you can sell someone else on massage therapy. And the fact is, you ARE a salesperson whether you think you are or not. So practice that elevator speech until you can say it anywhere, anytime, and in front of anyone.

Once you've perfected that you need to zero in on the target clientele most likely to use and appreciate the services you provide. Know which niche(s) you want to focus on and then direct your marketing efforts toward the groups of people that can benefit most from what you have to offer. Use as many different promotional techniques as you need to in order to keep your name in front of those interested in what you do, and who are ready to utilize your services. Be strategic in how you plan and implement your marketing. Write down the targets you will aim for each day, week, and month. Assess monthly how your promotional methods are working and make changes accordingly. Don't be afraid to try new marketing techniques. Think outside the box! Many times the most creative marketing methods are the ones that make you stand out from the crowd.

Most importantly, be consistent with your efforts. Marketing may not be everyone's favorite, but depending solely on word-of-mouth advertising, a business sign, or a listing in the phone book cannot produce a wildly successful practice.

Massage Marketing Schedule

The massage marketing schedule below is a simplified example of what a therapist might employ on a daily, weekly, and monthly basis to promote business.

Daily:

- Call and confirm client appointments for the next day.

- Make follow-up calls to new clients and at least one call to prospective clients.

- Invite scheduled clients to take brochures, business cards, or other materials to give to family, friends, and co-workers. Remind them of any referral incentives you offer.

Weekly:

- Stay in touch with at least one existing networking partner (doctor or chiropractor office, complementary health-care practitioner, etc.) or one joint-venture partner (hair salon, health-food store, gym, etc).

- Practice your elevator speech in public settings, especially those places that cater to your niche.

- Hand out ten business cards.

- Send handwritten thank-you notes or birthday cards to clients.

Monthly:

- Make contact with one new networking or JV partner.

- Attend a business-networking group function.

- Mail or e-mail a client newsletter.

- Prepare for an upcoming special offer or holiday promotion.

- Research upcoming health fairs or trade expos to attend.

- Review your marketing goals and techniques to assess what's working and what's not.

11 Give Your Business a Web Presence

Why do you need an online presence? Because the Internet is the primary resource people use to find out what they need to know. The Internet is one-stop shopping for information, products, and services. It quickly and efficiently answers the questions of "who, what, where, why, and how." In seconds and from the convenience of their own home or office, people can find millions of results in response to what they are looking for. And with mobile devices information can be obtained anywhere and anytime.

Using the Internet as a portal to your business gives the public a way to know you before ever meeting you in person. Many practitioners erroneously believe that all an Internet presence means is building a website. To effectively establish your brand or professional image, educate the public, and attract prospective clients you must take a multifaceted approach to online marketing. There are many ways of building an online presence to increase your visibility, but remember there are billions of pieces of information out there in cyberspace. You will need to find the methods that best serve your business and learn to use them well in order to get your business seen.

Many people are hesitant to use the Internet as part of their marketing plan due to lack of knowledge or skill, but in today's world it's not an option, it's a necessity. As a salesperson for yourself and your business, you must follow the trends that work. So get to know your Internet options, learn how to talk about what you do, and then get familiar with the techniques of search engine optimization, keyword use, viral marketing, and social networking. The more you know about Internet marketing and how to use it most effectively, the greater your online presence will be.

Building a Website

If you're not totally computer and Internet savvy, building a website from scratch will likely seem a foreign language to you. Fortunately, there are myriad options for site builders that can pretty much do the work for you by providing (or allowing you to choose) your own domain name, a hosting service, and all the components and features that you can simply click to add to your site.

The domain name will usually be the name of your business and it is what a reader will click to peruse your website. The hosting service is where the information on your website is contained.

Though there are many free website-hosting options, most experts will advise against using these because of the lack of freedom you get with them. For instance, free services provide a sub-domain name that is usually longer and more difficult for a user to remember, because instead of just your chosen domain name it will also include the name of the hosting site as well. Another aspect to consider with free hosts is that many will display unsightly ads on your website pages. We've all seen the flashy, animated banner ads that display across the top of a web page. Unless you're on a really fixed budget, this is not something you'll want your readers to see when they visit your site. And lastly, free hosting doesn't get the technical support that paid hosting does.

But although a free hosting service is not advisable, there are also hosting services with exceptional site builders that have variation in pricing for any budget. These are clear cut and most will say exactly what is included in each package.

Researching site builders is an intimidating option because there are so many. Oftentimes massage therapists and other bodyworkers will opt for those who cater specifically to their field. Although often a bit more costly, these can be tailored especially for the bodywork profession to include soothing backgrounds and graphics, easy-to-use templates to create web pages within the site, storefronts to sell products or gift certificates, and client schedulers.

The best advice is to research several, ask other practitioners who they use, and check out some of the actual websites created by these hosting sites and builders before making your final choice.

Getting Your Website Found

Hurrah! You've got a website. You've added a visitor counter and you check it every day but it's not moving. What? You thought all you had to do was build it and they

Basic Pages to Add to a Massage Therapy Website

This depends largely on the site builder you choose and the number of pages it allows on your website, but here are some basics you'll want:

- **Home page:** This is the page a reader will land on when they type in your URL (uniform resource locator, aka your website address). Here you will catch your reader's eye with inviting graphics and snippets of information about you and your business. This will also include your business location, hours of operation, and contact information.

- **Services:** Dedicate a page to listing what type of services you offer. You may have a list of several bodywork modalities (types) or just one. No matter how many or how few, give your services their own page. Include a bit of information on what each type of massage or bodywork entails and how it can benefit the reader.

- **Rates:** It's optional to have a rates page. If you have space, go ahead. If not, simply add the rates to your services page.

- **Policies:** This page states the terms and policies implemented in your business.

- **Massage benefits and FAQs:** These can be separate pages or combined. Explain to the reader in easy to understand language how massage can help them. Include answers to some of the more frequently asked questions people have such as "Will I be covered?" and "Do I have to take all my clothes off?" Make the tone of this page courteous, professional, and friendly. Don't use terminology that the lay person may not understand like "occipital ridge" or "palpation." (The occipital ridge is the base of the skull and palpation is assessment through touch.) Students are often chastised in school for not using proper terminology and it IS appropriate to know. But save it for your colleagues and others in the medical field, not your clients or readers of your website. If you do use any of these terms, explain briefly what they mean.

Optional pages if package allows:

- A "specials" page noting any discounts or holiday promotional material.
- Products sale page
- Client scheduler page

would come? Wrong. Just like a massage therapy license doesn't get clients coming to your door, neither does building a website get readers to it.

> *Getting readers to your site depends on one factor and one factor only: reaching the top of the search engine listings.*

This is where search engine optimization comes into play. Search engine optimization, or SEO, is the technology you use to improve your ranking in the major search engines such as Google, Bing, or Yahoo!.

Although there are three major criteria for a high-ranking website, the No. 1 criterion for improving your ranking is high-quality content. You have a massage therapy business so guess what your website should include lots of information on? You guessed it: massage therapy. OK, so that seems easy enough. But what's next?

Next comes how to use keywords. Keywords are the words or phrases a casual reader would use to search for your website information. "Massage therapy," "massage therapist," or "masseuse" are all examples of words someone might type in looking for massage. They might type in "massage in (city name)," so these words or terms would be considered keywords.

There are some great keyword tools on the Internet to help you choose the keywords most appropriate for your website but the best thing is to write good-quality content based on the topic you know: massage therapy. Overuse of the keyword tools may lead to keyword stuffing (using an excess of keywords to manipulate a website's rank to the point that the writing is poor quality). Keyword stuffing is considered unethical and may result in repercussions. Don't do it.

And finally, backlinks. Backlinks are those websites that link back to your site. Search engines use the number of these backlinks to improve your rank. The premise is if lots of people are linking to your site, it must be great! And if it's great, it deserves to rise in the search-engine listings. The caveat here is that the backlinks should be as high a quality as possible and relevant to the content your website provides.

If you want to have a basic website that your existing clients and customers can use, then you needn't bother with learning SEO. But if you want a website to drive traffic TO your business, then educating yourself on SEO practices or hiring someone to do an SEO campaign for you is necessary.

Reader searches are frequently done on businesses in particular areas. Making use of Google Places may be a wise decision as a service-oriented business that relies heavily on local patronage. Anyone can have their own Place page where they can list information on their business offerings, location, hours, photos and videos, and reviews of your business imported from review sites.

It's essentially another website for your business and you should treat it as such by updating and monitoring it frequently and managing the reviews, both good and bad, if any. In terms of SEO value, Google Place pages are ranked high on the search engines so even though a reader may never get past your Place page to click on your website link, you'll still get exposure for your business because it's unlikely that your website will rank as high. Don't forego building a website because of this. Some people want a lot more information before they make a decision—that's where your website comes into play. Use all the tools at your disposal.

Blogging for Business

Although blogs are technically websites, a standard website is updated with far less frequency than a blog. Usually a blog is updated daily or every other day. With either you can get free or variable-cost hosting service, but as stated earlier, free hosting is usually not the best choice.

Updating blog content is fast, easy to do, and indexed in search engines more quickly than most website content. Like websites, a blog can be monetized to earn money and because you can easily maintain your own, you needn't pay someone to update it regularly as you would for a website if you couldn't do it yourself.

Typically, blogs are well liked by search engines presumably because the content is constantly being refreshed and search engines appear to love fresh content. This means that good material added frequently, in combination with keywords and key-word phrases for SEO, are more likely to get your listings on the first one or two pages of major search engines.

Perhaps the biggest disadvantage to blogging is the need for new content on a regular basis. You must be prepared to put in the time to update with new posts daily or every other day, minimal. If you won't be able to do that, you can hire freelancers to

Google Adsense

By signing up for the Google Adsense program, you can earn revenue from your website or blog by allowing relevant ads to be placed on your pages. Each time an ad is clicked on by a reader, you can earn money.

write content for you based on your specifications. If you can't do either, build a basic website and utilize Google Places instead.

The distinction between blog and website is that a blog is interactive due to the dialogue between the blogger and the reader. This makes keeping a blog updated regularly invaluable by encouraging readers who follow it to visit more often and interact by reading and adding their own comments. A blog's unique value is its easy-going nature. It's quite similar to having a casual conversation with a friend, which may be, in part, why blogs are so popular. Combine this friendly, casual approach with the ease of connecting blogs to social networks and you can see why blogging is the current favorite of online content providers.

What are Tags?

Tags are labels that help to identify certain information. If you write a blog post called "massage therapy for stress reduction" some tags you might use for the post are "stress," "massage," "massage therapy," and "relaxation." These labels help to categorize blog posts and assist readers in finding relevant information faster.

Some blogs use a term called "tag clouds," which are groups of tags with the most popular or frequently used ones in larger, bolder font.

Social Networking

Social networking is groups of like-minded individuals connecting with one another. Online networks are common and link any type of group from hobby enthusiasts to business professionals. Although social networking groups exist in face-to-face settings, never have they been as popular as they are in the Internet community. This may be because of the ease of access through a computer or mobile device, lack of need for face-to-face interaction, or simply the savings of time and effort in comparison to the in-person meeting. Social networking has become a phenomenon that is sometimes called a fad but is more likely a look at the future and how people will connect and interact with one another for years to come. With traditional advertising like radio ads, yellow pages, and other print options becoming outdated and less effective as marketing strategies, it's probably fair to say that if you don't ride the social media wave, your business may get left behind.

Here is a look at a few of the top networking sites currently in use:

Facebook

Facebook is a social-networking site with millions of users worldwide. It was co-created by college students for other students to interact with one another. It grew far beyond all expectation and now connects friends, families, community members, business associates, and everyone in between. Connections are built through creating personal or business profiles, building friend lists, interacting on one another's walls and through private messages and chat, and on business pages. Business users can advertise through Facebook as a way to reach more of the public as well.

A distinct advantage to using Facebook as part of your marketing toolbox is that in less time, you can reach countless more people than you could canvassing the community, posting literature, and handing out business cards. And by simply adding the Facebook NetworkedBlogs application, you can set it up so your blog posts are automatically posted on Facebook as well. It's far less costly than advertising in the local newspaper and because you have a home-based practice, you may have available time in between clients to get online and make Facebook contacts or create or update your business page.

Many people see Facebook as something that is here today, gone tomorrow. But right now, Facebook is hot and never has there been an easier, less expensive way to get information on your massage business out to the people who need and want it most.

LinkedIn

Another social-networking platform is LinkedIn. LinkedIn is a professional networking site that helps users to build contact networks of colleagues and those people in related professions. LinkedIn can put users in touch with potential employers, employees, job listings, and other business opportunities through those connections.

As a massage therapist, you can not only make connections with other professionals but also receive advice and answers to your questions from experts in the massage therapy field.

Pinterest

Pinterest is a social media site that uses a visual concept consisting of "pin boards" and social interaction. Pin boards are digital bulletin boards that users can collect, organize, and store images and video to. These images can be saved for future viewing and sharing. Similar to other social networks, Pinterest uses a system of "followers" and "following" for users to interact with one another. With Pinterest's explosive growth, massage therapists may be wise to enlist it as yet another way to drive traffic to their websites or blogs, being aware that high-quality images are essential to generate the interest of viewers and increase the likelihood of being shared.

What kind of images might be effective? For a service-based business like massage, video clips of a massage in progress or demonstration of particular techniques would be ideal. Other interesting visuals might contain holistic health, spa, relaxing ambience, or nature imagery. These images can be your own (with links back to your blog) or they can be images you collect from around the Internet linking back to the original content owner. (Never simply pin Internet images without backlinking to the original owner's content.)

Posting others' content, in addition to a modest amount of your own, serves a dual purpose: 1) It lets people know you are not purely promoting yourself, which is not proper "netiquette," and 2) it shows your followers your commitment to the health and wellness industry.

Pinterest can be shared easily on Facebook and Twitter, and a "pin it" button can be added to your website and blog so readers can pin (share) your content.

Twitter

Twitter is a cross between microblogging (called "tweeting") and social networking. From a business perspective, it can be used to update followers with short snippets of educational information on massage therapy, specials, or discounts you're offering, or even when you have appointments available. Again, Twitter can be a distraction and time waster if you're not careful. Make your postings short, sweet, and to the point. Discipline yourself to post about business-related matters only so that you are associated solely to massage in the eyes of your followers. Tweet your website information but don't overdo promotion of your business. Keep a good balance of promoting and giving your followers useful information to keep them interested.

Internet Article Writing

Publishing online content is a way to establish your credibility within your field. Writing articles that may get reposted time and again can spread your expertise worldwide and increase your exposure exponentially. Many e-zine and blogsite owners welcome guest blogger articles, which make an excellent option to create visibility through sites other than your own. Research health-related niche sites and contact the owners to ask if you can post a relevant article to their blog or e-zine.

Many of the other e-zine websites you can sign up for have a "free to re-print" policy so if you submit an article to one of these sites, other websites and blogs can use that article you wrote and actually promote you to their readers without you needing to do anything further. Content is nearly always re-published with the

Sample Article

(Reprinted from my blog at http://journeysofmindbodyandspirit.blogspot.com)

How Can Massage Help?

Being a licensed massage therapist for the past ten years, I have heard a lot from people on what they think massage is like and how it benefits the body/mind. Some of the information is spot-on and some of it is most definitely lacking.

For instance, far too many people associate massage with this luxurious service that only pampered, rich people (who don't need it) can afford to get. Well, they're right that it can be luxurious, but it's not just for the spoiled set.

Massage therapy is highly beneficial for relieving the effects of everyday stress. Whether that stress load comes from work or family obligations, ill-health, relational difficulties, or any other situation, massage can effectively reduce (and relieve) the body and mind with the very first session. Why is this important? With stress linked to nearly every disease known to man, keeping it to a minimum may be a secret to a longer, healthier life.

Beyond stress relief, massage is frequently used for pain control, to release muscle tension, and speed injury rehabilitation. When used regularly, it is effective for headache-, shoulder-, and back-pain relief.

Massage works on all the systems of the body, not just the muscles. It rejuvenates the entire body by increasing the blood and lymph circulation. Oxygen is much more effectively distributed and utilized as well.

The skin brightens and internal organs become more toned. Certain massage techniques benefit the digestive tract and may curb constipation or symptoms of irritable-bowel syndrome. The nervous system is positively impacted and a release of "feel-good chemicals" is allowed to flood the body.

Now, with all that said, is massage therapy a panacea for every ailment out there? No. It does not suit all conditions, nor does everyone respond well to it. However, it IS another tool to use to increase the quality of your life. Give it a try. Your body and mind will thank you.

original author's name and bio so the more your articles get reposted elsewhere on the Internet, the more visibility for you and your business.

This may seem meaningless. You might be saying, "Why would I want someone in California reading my article on relaxation through massage when I live and practice in Georgia? How will that help me get business?" It won't directly. What it WILL do is establish you as an expert in the massage field. In turn, this will be helpful when you want to promote locally because you can let prospective clients know they can read about you and any articles you've published. As well, the more relevant articles you publish that are spread around the Internet, the more traffic gets driven back to your website, and the more easily you will be found in the search engines. Because of the trend in how people search now (via the Internet), being found in the search engines is of major importance to Internet marketing planning.

To write articles for content e-zines or other publications, write about what you know. You're a licensed massage therapist. You are an expert on stress relief and reducing pain. Pick certain topics and write a 500-word piece on each one. Be specific. One can be on tips for relieving stress at the holidays while another could address massage therapy for chronic pain sufferers. Make articles informative and useful. The more unique the content is, the better. Learn how to use keywords and search engine optimization most effectively so your articles don't get lost in cyberspace. Once you've learned SEO, remember your integrity and forego keyword stuffing. Make your writing informative and useful, mainly evergreen (relevant over a period of time), and readable.

Online Professional Directories

An online directory listing is very similar to a standard phone-book listing. There are thousands of online directories to choose from under the headings of massage therapy or healing arts. These directories are usually free to list in and will include your business name, contact information, and types of massage therapy you provide. Massage provider directories are also offered by the major professional massage organizations like American Massage Therapy Association (AMTA) and Associated Bodywork and Massage Professionals (ABMP).

With so many free massage therapist directories available, there is no need to pay for this service. Type "online massage directories," "free massage directories," or something similar into the search box and go through the first page or two of each directory to decide which sites might be most appropriate for your business listing.

Most will require you to sign up for an account before you can submit data about your business.

Video Marketing

Video is a form of marketing that is becoming more and more advantageous as part of your overall marketing strategy. With the popularity of websites like YouTube, videos have become a highly recognizable method to market products and services and provide educational information. Video marketing appeals to visual and auditory learners who may struggle with reading or comprehending the written word and to those who simply enjoy video content over written material. Videos also allow a viewer to feel he is meeting the person speaking, which creates both a sense of familiarity and more of a chance that the viewer will buy what the seller has to offer. Making connections that build trust and credibility through video marketing can help to further brand you as an expert in the massage therapy field.

With most social networking sites having share options available, videos have a strong likelihood of being passed around—viral marketing—which can make them a highly effective way to promote your business at a faster rate than with the use of other methods. Besides having the potential to be shared more frequently than written articles, the great thing about videos for marketing is that a thirty-second to one-minute video shot with a cell phone, basic video, or digital camera can be easily, inexpensively, and quickly posted. Video no longer needs to be professionally done to be effective. Even lower-quality video, if it has excellent content and appeal, has a very good chance of going viral and getting your message out there as readily as one that takes more to produce.

How Will You Get Exposure?

Building a web presence in today's business world is imperative in order to be seen and recognized as an expert in your profession. Because of the exposure to billions of people worldwide, you have the unique opportunity to put your name and face in front of them more easily and at record speed compared to other marketing methods.

Start this phase of your marketing plan with building a business website and a blog. As noted above, you can have one or the other, but for optimal effectiveness, both are best. Once these are in place, add high-quality content. Keep your posts pertinent to one topic each and add to them at regular intervals. Build up a base of followers (readers). After establishing your website and blog, add your business-contact information to online directories so that anyone looking for massage in your area will have you at their fingertips.

Add in article writing and share what you know with the public. Write about stress and what it does and how you can counter it, back pain and how to alleviate it, headaches and how massage can keep them under control, or life's difficulties and what can be done to manage them most effectively while staying calm. Make a list of potential topics. Start with topics you know very well and write about those first. Then move on to other topics you know somewhat, or are interested in, and research them well before writing them. Always make your writing accurate, clear, concise, and helpful to the reader. With any writing you do, be sure to use your own words and voice. Never plagiarize (copy) content from another writer unless you have express written consent to use it.

Lastly, consider video marketing. Video allows you to create simple content, upload it to the Internet, and have it viewed by people interested in the topic your video is about. Think about the message you want to put out to the viewers and create a few practice videos. Remember that these clips need only be a minute or less to extend a compelling and memorable message to your viewers.

Whatever online marketing tools you use to promote your expertise and grow your business, you must learn the search engine optimization techniques that will drive viewer traffic to read your website or blog, watch your videos, and ultimately note you as the massage expert they want to do business with. Before jumping in, research SEO production of quality Internet content and monetization of any sites you build that can be developed as a secondary source of income.

12 Growing Your Business

Where do you envision your business in five years? Look back over your business plan and the goals you set for the long term. What denotes success to you? Is it staying small and continuing to offer first-rate, personalized service to your clientele? Does it mean subcontracting other massage therapists to do the hands-on massage work while you attend to the task of running the business? Is it adding one or more product lines to enhance a thriving bodywork business or to assist you in reaching a certain income level? Only you can determine what it will take to satisfy you in terms of defining success. If you take the risk to grow your business, you will also feel trepidation along the way. You can never know when changes that negatively affect your business will occur. You can only try to foresee and safeguard against economic downturns, drops in clientele, and other situations to the best of your ability and press forward in whatever manner befits your needs best.

On-Site Work

As discussed in chapter 2, on-site massage work can be a change from the possible stagnation of working in a home office or studio all the time. It is also a good way to choose specific venues to work in such as schools, businesses, or doctors' offices. In the first few years I was building my practice, I contacted the local schools and doctors' offices to offer my services. At a fee of one dollar per minute, I could effectively see six people for ten minutes of seated-chair massage during a lunch hour. This was very convenient for the full-time employees who found it difficult to fit massage in at other times. A simple letter to the office manager or human resources person explaining who I was, what I offered, and how much it would cost was all that I needed to introduce myself and my services. I also chose to educate the person I was addressing with an explanation of how offering massage therapy would benefit their business by increasing the productivity of employees. Once hired, I arranged to come in one or two days per week through the lunch hour. Because it was scheduled, it was easy to work in around the clients I saw in my office. Although sometimes the clients paid for their own massage, oftentimes the management or the school's parent organization would pay for the employee's massage as a benefit to the job. An added bonus to the variety and pay of on-site work is that many of these employees, once they've experienced the effects of seated massage, will want to book further sessions in your home office. When used effectively on-site massage is also a promotional tool to generate new business for your home-based massage practice.

Subcontracting Massage Therapists

First of all, subcontracting is very different from having employees. A subcontractor is a self-employed individual who pays a percentage of income or a flat fee to you as the owner of your home-based business in exchange for use of massage space.

The independent subcontractor provides massage for her own clientele using her rules of conduct and methodology of practice. She is responsible for paying her own taxes, personal, property, and liability insurances, licensing, and other expenses. The subcontractor also attends to all of her own business marketing and promotion.

The business owner is responsible for costs related to the building—in this case the home massage office—such as heating, electricity, insurance, etc. She too pays her own taxes and all business-related expenses.

The reasons for hiring subcontractors are numerous but are mainly associated with saving money and avoiding the extra work of being an employer. With having subcontractors a business owner doesn't have to deal with hassles such as paying taxes and doing payroll. She has only to provide space, organize the days and times of use, collect her fee, and maintain her own business—not that of those who subcontract for her.

It is important to know the distinction between employee and subcontractor status in your state. Consult with the Small Business Association, the Internal Revenue Service, or an attorney regarding regulations in your locale to familiarize yourself with the differences and avoid potential infractions of the law.

Hiring Massage Therapy Marketing Specialists

Your home-based business may have reached the point where you are now able to hire others to do some of the regular marketing and promotional work. If so, congratulations! Consistently searching for the targeted audience most likely to use your services and then promoting yourself to them is a good part of your workweek, and delegating it to someone more experienced might be well worth the money. Keep in mind also that you can barter marketing services for massage therapy and use the cost of the exchange for tax purposes.

When enlisting the services of any marketing specialist—online or off—ask to see samples of their work before you hire them. Determine for yourself if the samples would compel you to buy the product or services being promoted. If not, keep looking until you find a marketer's work that does.

(Note: A marketing specialist may be different from a marketing consultant. Get to know anyone you are considering and make sure you are getting what you think you are. Some consultants may only assist you in finding and utilizing the optimal market-ing strategies for your business but will leave the actual work of making contacts and promoting up to you, where other specialists might attend to all details, upon your approval of any marketing strategies.)

Offline Marketing Specialists

An offline marketing specialist will assist you with direct marketing efforts based on the short- and long-term goals you've set for your business. Direct marketing will address many facets of marketing including finding your target market, copy-writing, and graphic design for your promotional literature. Many direct marketers will be companies with a full range of services, and others may specialize in one area or another. All should give you a project proposal after adequate discussion of your needs, then give you a cost estimate based on your overall marketing plans and objectives.

Offline marketing enlists more traditional methods, such as direct mail, restau-rant placemat advertising, signage, television and radio promotions, and others. Many of these options now integrate offline with online strategies.

For massage, an offline marketing specialist may be especially helpful to a thera-pist in direct-marketing campaigns for sporadic use such as when to target a certain population (for example, sports enthusiasts, new mothers, or the elderly) using bulk mailings. These types of mailings can also be used to promote occasional sale events or an open house.

Pay particular attention to the copywriting aspect of your strategies. Copy is promotional material in the form of sales letters, brochures, direct mailings, online content, press releases, etc., that paint a picture through words of why a customer should buy what you're selling, be it a service or a product. Copy is important because it must accomplish the following:

- **Draw the reader's attention with a compelling headline.** ("Buy one massage, get one free!")
- **State what the offer is and who it's from.** ("Therapeutic massage by a licensed, reputable massage therapist")
- **Give reasons why prospects should choose you by first appealing to their emotions, then logical reasoning.** (Emotions: "You feel bad because you want to play with your grandchild when she pleads with you while visiting, but you just don't have the energy and stamina. It's so hard to see the disappointment on her little face when you have to tell her grandma is just too tired." Logic: "Because the effects are cumulative, you will see your stress levels lowered and energy increased within one month of receiving weekly massage!")
- **Give the reader an enticing and urgent reason to buy now.** ("Buy one, get one offer won't be available again this year so NOW is the time to stock up on gift certificates for your friends, family, and yourself!")

"What's in it for me?" is what a reader of any copy wants to know. The benefits must be clear and compelling with an offer that instills a sense of urgency to buy. Keep these aspects in mind any time you create promotional material intended for distribution to your target market. Address the reader's needs in a strong way to see the biggest return on your direct marketing investment in both time and expense.

Online Marketing Specialists

As noted earlier, because a large segment of the population uses the Internet to find a business, online marketing strategies should be implemented with any other techniques in a business marketing plan. It differs from the offline marketing venue only because it uses the Internet via e-mail, web content, websites and blogs, online ads, and other sales pieces to direct consumers to do business with you.

Just as with direct marketing through standard methods like brochures and postal service bulk mailings, an online marketing campaign must use excellent copy to draw readers to buy the services and products you're selling. If the content of the copy is weak and doesn't address the four points made above, then the marketing efforts will be less effective in increasing business or sales. Use effective online copy to draw the buyer's attention, tell him what you're selling (massage therapy and related products), explain just how it will benefit him, and give him a specific call to action (buy now and tell him why he should).

Online marketing is somewhat tricky due to the ease of use of computer or other digital device keys and click factor of the Internet. Basically with web content, if you don't grab a reader's attention, she's off and running to the next page. In mere seconds, your information is lost in a sea of billions of other pieces of information scattered throughout the Internet.

Internet massage promotional information must always include headlines that catch (and hold) the reader's eye, testimonials for what you're promoting, massage facts and other educational materials, and persuasive reasons to buy and buy NOW.

Article Writing

Writing online content for your own websites, blogs, e-zines, or for other people's sites can be time consuming. Many massage therapists will get to this point in this chapter and say, "Wait a minute. If I do all this writing and promotional stuff, how will I ever have time to do what I love to do?" The answer to this is simple time management. Marketing isn't optional and one of the best ways to promote you and your business is by putting content out to massage consumers. The more useful educational material available, the more you stand out from the crowd as an expert in your field, and the one a consumer is more likely to contact for their massage therapy needs.

Another great aspect to writing content is the potential to earn additional income. I began my secondary career as a freelance writer simply by having the initial desire to communicate with and educate my clients about massage therapy and other ways to maintain or improve their health. I found sending e-mails or standard-mail newsletters very time consuming and came across a well-known website on which I could post my articles. I found that not only did I now have a central location to refer clients to, but I also developed a viable income source through earning residuals (residual income is income that you do the work once and get paid for repeatedly). In time, I found similar freelancing opportunities and now write on a variety of topics.

Once you begin to excel at it, writing an article of about 500 words can take less than fifteen minutes or up to an hour depending on the subject content. But for those who don't want to or can't write their own materials, there are other ways to access usable content.

Freelance or Ghost Writers

There might come a time when you want to outsource (hire out) your online content. The good news is that there is a multitude of talented freelance writers out there who would be eager and very well qualified to write your articles for you for a fee. Most freelancers are well-versed in researching topics with which they are less familiar. And ultimately you have the final word on what elements the content must contain in order to meet your project specifications. Freelance writers are readily available for occasional work as well as for regularly contributed articles needed for blog or e-zine content. When hiring a freelancer to write content for you, the ownership of the content becomes yours and should be so stated in any agreement you have.

PLR (Private Label Rights) Articles

PLR content is material sold to the public and can be edited to any degree the buyer needs to suit her needs and labeled under a private label as her own content.

You can simply type in your niche ("massage") and "PLR articles" to check out the web pages that show up. Read over some of the work and determine if the cost and quality suits your needs before buying content.

After purchase, PLR articles can be placed on websites, in blogs, e-zines, and other web or offline materials. Once PLR content is purchased, it becomes the property of the buyer. The issue with PLR articles is they can be sold to more than one buyer, which negates the concept of original content. Many websites on which you place content will specify original content only (meaning they don't want the same article on their website that is on ten other websites) so the PLR article needs to be altered significantly in order to be considered original. This may not pose a problem for you if you want to put it on your own website or blog. However, remember that beyond promoting your business, your goal is to market your expertise in the massage therapy field. If you buy and publish PLR articles under your name that are already on the Internet without altering them considerably, your credibility may suffer. Another consideration for PLR articles is rights of ownership. Always check to make sure you have full right to use and alter the article before you put your name on it.

Add-On Services

Offer clients an extra service tacked on to their regular massage that you know will benefit them. For instance, a ten-to-fifteen-minute paraffin-wax hand dip treatment for someone with arthritic joints is an excellent adjunct to a massage session. An add-on treatment is beneficial in several ways: It provides increased value to address a client's session goals, it gives variety to a standard massage therapy session, and it offers you a way to earn more money. Add-on services make great gifts to reward clients for referring others to you, to recognize special occasions, or as a prompt for gift certificate sales.

Product Sales

Many times a massage practitioner will use products in her office that a client will enjoy and want to have for home use. Initially, you may not want to invest in these products to sell in your office. However, it would be wise to take note of anything that seems to be popular and requested frequently because there may come a time when you have the income and desire to make the products available for sale. Keep in mind that not only can product sales provide additional income, but having them readily available to a client who has expressed an interest and can then purchase on the spot, is another way of enhancing the client's experience. The key concept here is to believe in the products you sell so you don't look like a salesperson pushing your goods. And ultimately, you'll want to create a memorable experience for her so she'll be back for more.

Finding Products to Sell

If you are a home enthusiast with basic knowledge you can create some of your own products such as massage oils, bath salts and body scrubs, and herbal hot packs. The Internet has thousands of recipes and how-to instructions for making these products. Note that other than hot packs, most of these home made versions are made on demand—a client requests them and you make them. The reason for this is home made products are difficult to preserve and thus the shelf life is severely limited.

For those who cannot, or who choose not to, make custom products to sell, there are a number of wholesale massage and wellness-product suppliers on the Internet to choose from. A simple Internet search for "wholesale massage therapy products" will bring up plenty of websites Before you decide, be sure to choose products you would use in your massage practice. Then determine if they are popular enough with your clientele to purchase for resale.

Sample Product Ideas

- Oils
- Lotions
- Creams
- Body scrubs
- Hot and cold therapy packs
- Self-massage tools
- New Age music
- Meditation audios

Pricing Products

There is no definitive pricing structure that fits all products, but on average I charge three times what my total cost per product is. Obviously, the lower the total cost, the higher the profit. Here are the steps I take when I price the products I sell:

- Figure the actual cost plus tax per piece.
- Figure the shipping cost per piece.
- Add enough to make a profit (of my choice) after costs.

Other considerations when pricing a product include the following:

- If you buy local or pay to ship and how much each of those will cost
- Purchasing products versus making them (which you must then include cost of labor)
- What the local market is charging on similar products

Displaying Products

No matter how much or how little space you have in your home-based business, if you are selling a product you want to put it where a client can see it. This can mean anything from a simple shelf on the wall to an ultra-modern, lighted glass display case. If a client can see the product, she can ask questions about it. This is your opportunity to educate her on what it can do to benefit her.

But here is the secret: It's not enough to just place the products where she can see them. It doesn't matter how elegant or dressed up your display is to look at. The very simple fact is, you must USE the coconut-lime body scrub on your client or *demonstrate* the trigger point hand-held tool she can use on her neck at home to alleviate chronic headaches. Utilize as many of her senses as possible to make the sale. This means explaining what it can do to benefit her, demonstrating it, and allowing her to see and touch it for herself. Finally, be OK with it if she decides not to purchase at this time. Look at it as refining your skills at selling your products and yourself.

Joining an Existing Practice

There may come a time when the home-based business model no longer suits your needs and you have a desire or need to join an existing practice. Because by now you already know the genre of people you enjoy working with and the type of massage and bodywork you choose to employ, and you should be able to readily identify the workplace options you may garner the most success in. Popular suggestions for massage therapy workplaces are medical spa facilities, day spas, physician's offices, chiropractor's offices, hair and tanning salons, and alternative health-care facilities. The benefits of joining an existing practice may include not having to deal with finding your own clients (marketing and promoting), scheduling, and cleaning. The disadvantages are the lack of overall freedom you had in your home-based practice and space-rental fees, or earning percentages you have to pay to the business.

Where Do You Want to Go?

When you consider your business "end game," it often comes down to wanting to make a concerted effort to work smarter, not harder. This concept may include having massage therapy subcontractors working for you, which can provide additional income and more publicity for your business without the responsibility of being an employer.

On the basis of working smarter, hiring experts in the field of marketing may be a viable option for you to promote your business without having to do the work it entails. An important point stated earlier bears repeating: Marketing isn't an option. Marketing is a necessity. It isn't something done once or twice a year.

Key Business Concepts

- People will come to you because they have a problem that you can solve.

- Commit to excellence.

- Your No. 1 priority is meeting the client's goals and needs for each session.

- As your own boss, it's up to you to know the ever-changing tax laws in your state and adhere to them.

- Integrity and respect are building blocks for a solid ethical practice. You must do what you say you'll do, value your principles and stand by them, and respect yourself and your business, as well as the colleagues and clients you work with each day.

- Just as you have a toolbox of massage tools and techniques, so too should you have one prepared with fun, interesting, and inspiring options to use for regular self-care for your own mind, body, and spirit.

- As health-care providers, we spend a good part of our day taking care of others, making it vital that we also take care of our own well-being.

- You never get a second chance to make a first impression.

- Always put forth the extra effort needed to keep your space uncluttered, neutral, and professional looking.

- Regardless of the difficulty or ease of my day, I put on a smile as I speak so the client hears it in my voice.

- Be disciplined in the management of your time so that time doesn't manage you.

- If you can't sell yourself and your services, you have no business.

- It's far easier to keep an existing client than find a new one.

- The more you present yourself as a qualified health-care practitioner, the more likely you are to be seen that way.

- Learning from others who have done what you are setting out to do and tailoring that knowledge to suit your own needs is an integral part of making any business work.

- Perhaps most important are the concepts of a can-do mind-set and follow-through of action. Ultimately, if you know in your mind that you can succeed and you plan accordingly, you will find or make the opportunities to bring about that success. Planning is essential, yet it's inspired action that will take you where you want to go.

- Writing goals down on paper puts tangibility to your dreams and aspirations.

- Short-term goals should always be made with foresight in regard to how they relate to the longer-range goals. In other words, short-term goal setting should always be considered steps toward reaching long-range, or bigger, goals.

- Always keep your goals something to stretch for without making them so out of reach that you give up on attaining them.

- Be familiar with the laws regarding massage licensing in your state, if there are any, and always stay within the scope of your ability to practice.

- It is your responsibility to make sure you have all the receipts to back up any claims of income and expenses because the burden of proof is on you, not your accountant.

- When discounting is used effectively, it can be a great marketing tool. But regardless of why you do it, it's important to remember that discounting will ultimately affect your bottom line either by lowering the amount of income generated or by forcing you to work more hours to maintain a desirable income-to-expense ratio.

- You need an income to pay the bills, which will provide security, business growth, and success, but paying yourself first is what will give personal satisfaction and continued motivation to do what you do.

- Work smarter not harder.

- Focus on the potential for achievement, not fear of failure, and use the language of the successful to bring your definition of wealth to reality. Fill your mind and your life with positive thoughts, statements, and actions to develop a wealth mind-set.

Promoting you and your business needs to be done consistently and the results measured for effectiveness on a regular basis. This is no small task, which is why many massage therapists only market sporadically, if at all.

Many massage therapists are terrified at the concept of online marketing. Yet ask just about anyone you know where the first place they go to find information and they will likely tell you the Internet. At a viewer's fingertips is everything he needs to find the people, places, products, services, businesses, and educational material he's searching for. But because it's so simple to click away from a page, any content you post about your massage business must be relevant, current, eye-catching, and compelling enough for a reader to not only read it, but save it to Favorites or share it through e-mail or social networking sites.

For the massage therapist who says, "I'm a bodyworker, not a writer!" outsourcing may be the key to adding regular online content that can be highly effective at establishing you as a one-stop source of massage information. Use outsourcing of article content judiciously, however. The content you post must always represent you, your beliefs, and ultimately, your business. Don't jeopardize your credibility by throwing out random content in an attempt to put quantity before quality.

A good working knowledge of search engine optimization (the techniques to boost your content to the first or second pages of major search engines) combined with excellent content is what will get your massage information seen above all the other content floating in cyberspace.

Another aspect of looking ahead to see what more you can add to increase your business and your income, is carrying products related to massage or wellness. These can include, but are not limited to, massage oils and lotions, handheld or percussion-type massage tools, or spa products. It is possible to buy quality wholesale items and mark them up adequately for resale. Though it's more of a challenge, it's also possible to create your own line of massage lubricants, herbal hot packs for pain relief, or spa-type products.

Many of the ideas in this chapter will come after you have built your business to a point where income and client numbers are steadily increasing. Consider that if you bring in subcontractors, there will need to be a great deal of clarity and communication for the business relationship to work. And when you add products you are responsible for ordering, stocking, selling, and learning about every product you sell. Always remember that the product represents YOU.

Finally, hiring marketing and freelance specialists is a great option to free up your time, but because the choices seem endless, it may not be an easy task to find the right experts to suit your needs at a price that also works. Researching the best deal is always part of working smarter, not harder.

Closing Thoughts

So here you are at the end of the road. Or is it the end? You may be nearing the end of the book, and I certainly hope you've gotten many ideas and pearls of wisdom from within. But you're nowhere near the end of your journey regardless of whether you're just considering massage or you are a veteran massage therapist.

Like many professions, a massage therapy career isn't easy yet unfortunately it's often painted as such. "Work part time for more than full-time pay!" "Provide relaxing massage in the comfort of your home and avoid the hassles of having a boss and nine-to-five hours!" "Earn $65 to $100 dollars per hour!" you'll see, hear, or read. Are these statements true? They can be, but they also aren't that simple. Massage therapy is a wonderful career choice for those who love working with their hands, love people, and love the healing professions. But massage income levels vary from city to city and state to state, so though the income potential is good, it's far from the idyllic picture often conveyed to the aspiring therapist-to-be. It's important to be realistic and realize that what a practitioner earns in rural Maine is not likely to be on par with what one earns in Las Vegas. And what one practitioner has for business expenses (overhead) may not compare to another's.

The bottom line is although being your own boss and creating a home-based massage therapy business from the ground up is exhilarating and satisfying, it's also challenging and disheartening at times. That's why you must know in your heart why you chose this profession and the home-based business model.

The great thing about being a massage therapist is opportunities are endless. You may have full intentions of working from home indefinitely but then find it no longer suits you at some point in time. You may eventually want to venture forth to medical facilities, spas, cruise ships, or other opportunities. The point is the massage field has no bounds in terms of opportunity. And just as the "where" is without limits, so is the "what." There are hundreds of types of physical and energetic bodywork. You can choose from those that are very physically challenging to those that don't require much physical exertion on the part of the practitioner.

But no matter where you choose to work or what type of massage or other bodywork that you provide, you must commit to doing it to the best of your ability. You are in the health-care profession and people will come to you because they have a problem that you can solve. What a concept! You can help the client who comes to you to relieve chronic anxiety due to work stress or provide massage therapy that improves mobility in an eighty-seven-year-old client who struggles to walk across the room. As a massage therapist you are changing someone's life every time you work with them so never take that responsibility lightly.

The following are a few simple suggestions that can further assist you in making your massage therapy dream rise far and beyond the lofty vision you had at its inception:

- **Cross-reference information.** When it comes to owning and operating a business, you need to know what you're doing to comply with local, state, and federal laws and regulations. If you belong to a professional massage organization, you must also comply with their regulations. Cross-reference all sources of information that you read or hear about for accuracy and compliance in your locale and for your particular business needs.
- **Do as you say.** Don't expect a client to be sold on the cumulative benefits of massage because you say so if you never take the time to have one yourself.
- **Continue learning.** Life is about expansion and it's imperative to learn something new regularly. The massage and bodywork field is growing exponentially. Hone your craft.
- **Commit to excellence.** When you commit to excelling at what you do, you become the reliable source that people will seek out when they need what you have to offer.
- **Work smarter not harder.** Never take five hundred steps to accomplish something when you can do it in fifty with the same, or better, results.

In closing, I would say it's probably unlikely that you got into massage or other bodywork strictly for the money or the opportunity to work from home, though those

may be contributing factors. Most likely, as with most healers, you chose massage
therapy to help others live a better life. And with the honor of helping others always
comes the unique opportunity to help oneself, so be your best, do your best, learn
from each mistake, and celebrate every success along the way!

Business

Internal Revenue Service

The IRS website contains links to all aspects of business and taxation. The small business and self-employed tab links to resources with forms, publications, and a selection of educational materials on owning and operating a small business.
www.irs.gov

Small Business Administration

The SBA assists business owners with all phases of business ownership from start to finish, including financing where applicable.
www.sba.gov

SCORE

SCORE is a not-for-profit group made up of volunteer business advisors. Online mentoring, face-to-face counseling, and online workshops are available.
www.sba.gov/content/score

Further Education

American Massage Therapy Association

The AMTA offers online or on-site continuing education opportunities for massage therapists to earn continuing education hours.
www.amtamassage.org/education/

Associated Bodywork & Massage Professionals

ABMP has an online education center for member use to earn continuing education hours.
www.abmp1.com

Cross Country Education

CCE offers educational opportunities in a wide range of professions including massage therapy. Courses are in several different formats with continuing education hours available.

www.crosscountryeducation.com

Erik Dalton

Dr. Dalton is a known leader in the massage and bodywork field. His website has an extensive selection of home-study courses, workshops, and educational DVDs available.

www.erikdalton.com

Get Body Smart

Get Body Smart is an online anatomy and physiology textbook using animated representations of the body systems for visual learning. Quizzes are included at each section end.

www.getbodysmart.com

InnerBody

InnerBody is an interactive anatomy website that utilizes animation, graphics, charts, and diagrams for study of the human anatomical structure.

www.innerbody.com

Real BodyWork

When clicking on the "Muscles" tab, a scroll listing of the muscular system is accessible. Each muscle group has graphics to show the muscle and a written description including names, function, and other pertinent information.

www.realbodywork.com

The Trigger Point Therapy Workbook: Your Self-Treatment Guide to Pain Relief

This is a comprehensive manual with full explanations and diagrams of trigger points, their locations, and how to treat them effectively by Clair Davies with Amber Davies.

www.triggerpointbook.com

Massage Equipment and Supplies

Biofreeze
www.biofreeze.com

Biotone
www.biotone.com

Bodywork Mall
www.bodyworkmall.com

Earthlite
www.earthlite.com

Massage King
www.massageking.com

Massage Table Superstore
www.massage-table-direct.com

Massage Warehouse
www.massagewarehouse.com

Oakworks
www.oakworks.com

Soothing Touch
www.soothingtouch.com

Office Equipment and Supplies

Costco
www.costco.com

Office Depot
www.officedepot.com

Office Max
www.officemax.com

Sam's Club
www.samsclub.com

Staples
www.staples.com

Professional Exams

Massage & Bodywork Licensing Examination
MBLEx is a national exam governed by the Federation of State Massage Therapy Boards. Exam content, application process, tutorials, FAQs, and a listing of states that accept the MBLEx are listed.
www.fsmtb.org

National Certification Examination for Therapeutic Massage (NCETM)
National Certification Examination for Therapeutic Massage & Bodywork (NCETMB)
NCETM and NCETMB are both NCBTMB certification exams. The major difference between the two is the NCETMB exam has questions on bodywork evaluation and implementation.
www.ncbtmb.org

Professional Liability Insurance
American Massage Therapy Association
www.amtamassage.org

Associated Bodywork & Massage Professionals
www.abmp.com

Hands-On Trade Association
www.handsoninsurance.com

Massage-Insurance.com
www.massage-insurance.com

National Association of Massage Therapists
www.namtonline.com

Professional Organizations

American Massage Therapy Association

AMTA is a professional organization dedicated to the continual striving for excellence and education in, and about, the massage therapy profession. The association serves massage schools, students, and licensed massage therapists.
www.amtamassage.org

Associated Bodywork & Massage Professionals

ABMP is a professional massage organization that serves over 79,000 members and provides an extensive liability insurance coverage and member benefits package.
www.abmp.com

Federation of State Massage Therapy Boards

The FSMTB is a federation representing several state boards that provides a licensing exam for the massage profession through administration of the MBLEx.
www.fsmtb.org

Foundation for Alternative and Integrative Medicine

FAIM searches out and conducts studies on alternative therapies. The organization then works with other health-care partners to verify the effectiveness and encourage the promotion and use of these often low-cost options.
www.faim.org

The Healing Touch Professional Association

HTPA is an organization that supports the growth of Healing Touch and the students, HT practitioners, and instructors who form the membership.
www.htprofessionalassociation.com

International Association of Infant Massage, Inc.

IAIMI is an international organization that trains certified infant massage instructors for the purpose of educating parents and other caregivers in massage techniques, and theory of, infant massage.

www.iaim-us.com

International SPA Association

The International SPA Association represents members in all areas of the trade from medical and day spa facilities to service providers such as massage therapists and other health-care practitioners.

www.experienceispa.com

National Certification Board for Therapeutic Massage & Bodywork

The NCBTMB provides a certification program for the purpose of upholding the highest standards of excellence for bodyworkers and the massage therapy profession. To become certified, a massage practitioner must have undergone a minimum massage course of 500 hours, demonstrate basic knowledge and skill, pass the national certification exam, follow the code of ethics and standards of practice as established by the NCBTMB, and commit to continuing education in order to be re-certified.

www.ncbtmb.org

Publications

Entrepreneur Magazine is a monthly publication for business owners and entrepreneurs. The magazine is subscription-based with print and digital editions.

www.entrepreneur.com

Massage and Bodywork Magazine is a subscription-based magazine with print and digital versions.

www.massageandbodywork.com

Massage Magazine is a subscription-based magazine with print and digital versions.

www.massagemag.com

Massage Today is a monthly publication that is free for practicing massage therapists or at a subscriber's fee for the public.
www.massagetoday.com

Trade Shows and Conventions

AMTA National Convention
www.amta.org

Florida State Massage Therapy Association Convention and Trade Show
www.fsmta.org

International SPA Association Conference and Exposition
www.experienceispa.com

World Massage Festival
www.worldmassagefestival.com

Appendix B: Massage Therapy Training and Certification

As with most professions, the massage therapy field is ever-changing. Laws and regulations are altered and upgraded frequently to raise the bar of professionalism and promote a higher level of excellence within the field. Therefore, just as it's critical to have a manager who oversees the functions of a store and its employees, it's equally important to have governing bodies that oversee the functions of the massage profession and its therapists at a state and national level.

To become a licensed massage therapist, you will complete or will have already completed a course of study and learned the hands-on skills to provide therapeutic massage in different settings. You likely will choose to become a member of a professional massage therapy organization. Participation in these organizations not only helps keep you abreast of changes in laws and regulations but is helpful in locating the resources you may need to further your training and education in the massage profession.

Your initial massage therapy education most often encompasses an introduction to many different bodywork modalities. This introductory training is designed to familiarize you with other types of bodywork beyond Swedish techniques, which are generally the foundation of your practice and educational background. But most likely, one aspect of your career as a massage therapist will be to continue to perfect your craft. This will entail taking continuing education classes, courses, and workshops. It may also consist of specializing in particular areas of the massage and bodywork profession. This appendix will provide a partial listing of other massage and bodywork modalities that you may, at some point in your career, want to add to your healing arts resume.

National Certification

The importance of national certification goes beyond the attainment of credentials. It denotes a strong commitment to professionalism and maintenance of the highest standards of excellence in your field.

To become nationally certified you must have completed a minimum 500-hour massage therapy course of study, show that you have the required foundational massage knowledge and technical skills, pass a national exam, commit to upholding the certifying body's code of conduct and professionalism, and earn continuing education credits in the massage (or related) field in order to remain certified.

The advantages of becoming nationally certified are numerous. First, it establishes you as a practitioner with the highest standards in your field. Being certified allows you a higher likelihood of employability in other states, a stronger degree of credibility among your clients and colleagues, and identifies you as a qualified health-care practitioner just like any other that requires certification at a national level.

The faster the massage field grows, the greater your competition. National certification can also give you an edge over that competition and firmly establish your reputation as an accomplished massage therapist or bodyworker.

Continuing Education

The health-care field is always changing. Methods are streamlined, new techniques learned, and technology advanced. The massage therapy and bodywork profession is ever changing too. Once considered only a luxurious treatment to pamper oneself with, massage has grown by leaps and bounds to encompass not only pampering but also to be recognized as an effective option to facilitate healing of the body. Massage therapy is performed in the home office, spas, medical facilities, and locker rooms. It addresses stress, strain, anxiety, pain, depression, effects of cancer, cardiovascular conditions, and other disease of the body. Massage has moved far beyond the confines of being only for the spoiled and rich. Because of this growth, continuing education in the field is of great significance. From the home-massage office setting to the hospital setting, growing your practice is an ever-evolving process that includes maintaining skills and learning new ones.

As well as keeping up with changes in techniques, modalities, and massage treatment options for health conditions, continuing education is useful for renewing your interest in your profession. After years of being a massage practitioner, it becomes easy to grow complacent about your work. It becomes repetitive and may feel boring. Taking classes to learn new techniques or modalities can breathe new life into your practice and instill renewed excitement for you as a bodyworker.

Many regulatory boards now require CE (continuing education) hours to maintain licensure or national certification, so check at your local and state levels to determine what you need to be in compliance.

CE credit hours are available through workshops, classes at massage schools and colleges, online courses, webinars, and even through home video study. Always confirm with the course provider that the class you are receiving credits for is accepted as continuing education by your state massage board. To be considered acceptable, a class must be related to the massage and bodywork field. It can be classes on skills and techniques, but many business-related classes will qualify as well.

Specialization

Specialization in the massage field means gaining education in one particular area, or niche, of the healing-arts profession. Because specialists in most fields typically command a higher income, this may be a goal you set for your business. As with anything though, to label yourself as a specialist you must be certain you attain the skills, knowledge, and abilities to excel in the area you've chosen. You're no longer a general practitioner who meets standard skill levels, but one who has achieved greater proficiency in a specific area.

Many massage therapists will incorporate one or more specialty modalities into their existing practice simply to have more choices to offer clients. Others will be drawn to a particular field of study, such as shiatsu or myofascial release, and focus their practice on that.

BodyWork Modalities

Massage therapy and bodywork have a broad range of types, purposes, and differing populations who use them so there are any number of interesting choices for the practitioner who wants to specialize. On the following page is a sampling of the hundreds of practiced modalities in use today.

(Note: The following list is not comprehensive. It is a mixture of Western, Eastern, and energetic bodywork options you may wish to examine more closely as you develop your practice.)

- **Acupressure:** Acupressure is an Eastern bodywork practice that uses fingertip pressure applied at certain points of the body to release tension, increase circulation, and assist with balancing the body and improving or maintaining health.
- **Aromatherapy:** Often used as an adjunct to massage, aromatherapy is the science of using plant oils to elicit a healing response in the body and mind. Essential oils are extracted from plant-based materials and are most frequently used by inhaling, applying to the body through massage preparations, or diffusing into a room.
- **BodyTalk:** The BodyTalk system utilizes a process in which the body's systems reconnect and work in harmony with one another. Like other bodywork types, it can be used as a stand-alone system or in synergy with other healing modalities.
- **Craniosacral therapy:** Cranial-sacral work is manual therapy that gently assesses and improves the cranial-sacral system, which extends from the brain down the length of the spine to the tailbone. Using very light touch, the therapist tests for restrictions and assists with regulating the natural flow of spinal fluids.
- **Geriatric massage:** This type of massage specializes in working with the elderly. The work specifically addresses the particular needs of the aging population and may be provided in offices, homes, hospitals, or short- and long-term care facilities.
- **Infant massage:** Trained infant massage instructors teach parents and other caregivers how to massage their babies on an individual basis or in a classroom setting. Infant massage may also be employed in the hospital setting.
- **Manual lymph drainage massage:** Manual lymph drainage massage is a gentle, non-invasive manual therapy that uses precise, rhythmic strokes to improve lymphatic flow and stimulate toxin removal.
- **Myofascial release:** Using visual analysis and palpation techniques, a therapist notes areas of tension and applies gentle pressure to reduce or eliminate restrictions in the fascial tissues (fascial tissues, or simply fascia, are the connective tissues that bind the different structures of the body together).
- **Polarity therapy:** Polarity therapists use gentle, non-invasive manipulation of the body to balance positive and negative energies. Polarity therapy uses an integrated approach to health and healing, often incorporating the use of several bodywork modalities in a session.

- **Pre-natal massage:** Pre-natal, or pregnancy massage, provides gentle bodywork to address the changing needs of the pregnant female body throughout the stages of pregnancy and after birth.
- **Reflexology:** Similar in theory to acupressure, reflexology practitioners apply fingertip pressure to specific points that correspond to certain areas of the body. These points are located in zones on the feet, hands, and ears. The treatment is designed to relieve bodily congestion and facilitate balance within.
- **Reiki:** Reiki is a hands-on, energetic bodywork system originating in Japan. A Reiki practitioner channels healing life-force energy through the body using hand positions on, or just above the receiver's body. Reiki treatment helps balance the body, mind, and spirit.
- **Shiatsu:** An Eastern system, shiatsu uses finger, thumb, elbows, and palm pressure on particular points along the meridian systems of the body to facilitate self-healing in the receiver.
- **Sports massage:** Sports massage practitioners assist athletes and others who engage in sports on a regular basis to reach higher levels of performance. A therapist also provides results-based manual therapy for athletic injury and strain.
- **Therapeutic touch:** Frequently used by nurses and other practitioners in hospitals and various care settings, therapeutic touch is a gentle, touch-based bodywork in which a practitioner senses imbalances in the energetic structure and uses laying on of hands to resolve them. It is effective at inducing relaxation quickly and safely.
- **Zero balancing:** Zero balancing seeks to facilitate structural and energetic balance throughout the body by focusing on the bones of the skeletal system using acupressure-like touch.

How Will You Stay Current?

Throughout your massage and bodywork education, you will be encouraged heartily by your instructors to join one or more professional organizations to stay up to date on changes in the massage therapy profession. Further, you will be educated in the benefits of becoming nationally certified and hopefully setting yourself apart by keeping yourself informed, looking for new opportunities, and maintaining a sound level of professionalism and commitment to excellence with your clients, your colleagues, and the public. The more you present yourself as a qualified health-care practitioner, the more likely you are to be seen that way. This can help you not only in gaining credibility among other medical practitioners who may then refer patients to you but also as another voice to prompt more insurance companies to recognize massage therapy as a viable health and wellness choice.

As a health-care practitioner with high standards, you must also add continuing education to your overall business plan. Some massage organizations and state boards will require regular acquisition of CE credits and others will not. If not, it is up to you as a licensed practitioner to commit yourself to always improving your craft. Continuing education is readily available no matter where you're located with on-site, online, and even home-study options. Your only excuse for not furthering your education in the massage therapy field is you.

Participating in continuing education classes or learning entirely new bodywork modalities can rejuvenate a boring practice, add more income, and offer additional bodywork choices to clients.

Another aspect that practitioners may want to consider is that many long-term therapists find that extended hours of providing hands-on massage causes repetitive strain in finger and thumb joints, wrists, or shoulder joints. Many other bodywork or energetic therapies are very gentle on the practitioner and don't require forceful repetitive use. This should definitely be something to keep in mind when planning out your long-range goals. Adding, or changing, bodywork modalities can make the difference in your career life span.

Glossary of Abbreviated Terms

Organizations

ABMP: Associated Bodywork and Massage Professionals

AMTA: American Massage Therapy Association

FAIM: Foundation for Alternative and Integrative Medicine

FSMTA: Florida State Massage Therapy Association

FSMTB: Federation of State Massage Therapy Boards

IAIMI: International Association of Infant Massage, Inc.

HTPA: Healing Touch Professional Association

NCBTMB: National Certification Board for Therapeutic Massage & Bodywork

NCCA: National Commission for Certifying Agencies

Anatomy and Conditions Commonly Related to Massage Therapy

CFS: Chronic fatigue syndrome

CNS: Central nervous system

FM: Fibromyalgia

GAD: General anxiety disorder

GERD: Gastroesophageal reflux disease

HPB: High blood pressure

IBS: Irritable bowel syndrome

MS: Multiple sclerosis

OA: Osteoarthritis

PNS: Peripheral nervous system

PMS: Premenstrual syndrome

RA: Rheumatoid arthritis

SAD: Seasonal affective disorder

SI: Sacroiliac (referring to the sacroiliac joint)

SCM: Sternocleidomastoid

Bodywork Terminology

CAM: Complementary and alternative medicine

CARE: Client note charting system (condition, action, response, evaluation)

CMT: Certified massage therapist

CPT: Current procedural terminology used in health-care professions

CTM: Connective tissue massage

LDT: Lymph drainage therapy

LMT: Licensed massage therapist

MET: Muscle energy technique

NISA: Neuromuscular integration and structural alignment

NMT: Neuromuscular therapy

QT: Quantum-Touch

RICE: Rest, ice, compression, elevation

RMT: Registered massage therapist

ROM: Range of motion

SI: Structural integration

SOAP: Client note charting system (subjective, objective, assessment, plan)

STR: Soft tissue release

TP: Trigger point

Compression: Compression consists of palm pressure and holding to access and release constrictions in deeper muscles. The pressure begins lightly and increases slowly to deeper levels in order to reduce the likelihood of the muscle going into spasm or causing discomfort to the client.

Deep tissue: Though not a stroke per say, deep-tissue massage is using many of the aforementioned massage strokes at a deeper, more concentrated level. Deep-tissue work is designed to address adhesions (commonly known as knots) in the muscle layers to reduce pain and increase function.

Effleurage: A method of continuous gliding, or sliding, motions. The pressure is mild to moderately deep to encourage relaxation. Effleurage is a beginning stroke and is often used sporadically in between other deeper strokes to connect them and keep the flow of the massage continuous.

Feather stroking: This technique is typically a finishing stroke or one that is used in between deep pressured strokes. It is relaxing, calming and ideal for the elderly, ill, children, or others who require a lighter touch.

Friction: Friction typically denotes a rubbing over the muscle structures to create heat and increase circulation in an area without causing excessive discomfort to the skin surface. Friction can be applied in the direction of the muscles fibers or across.

Myofascial release: Without the use of oils or other lubricants, a practitioner elicits pain relief and increase in muscle function through slow, consistent pressure on myofascial restrictions. This is a stand-alone system or can be incorporated within a massage session.

Petrissage: This stroke is a kneading, lifting, and squeezing stroke often used on the bigger muscles of the arms and legs. When using petrissage the palms and finger pads should mold to the muscle and lift gently without pinching.

Tapotement: A stroke characterized by tapping, tapotement includes cupping, hacking, and other forms of percussive motions using the fingers, sides of the hands, closed fists, or cupped palms. (Some hand-held, battery, or electrically operated massage tools have a percussive function.)

Trigger point work: Trigger point therapy addresses tender nodules in muscle tissue. These nodules are active or latent. Active trigger points can refer pain elsewhere in the body. Latent ones hurt at the site of tenderness only. Therapy consists of fingertip pressure or the use of a hand-held tool to deactivate trigger points. See www.triggerpointbook.com for an excellent resource on self-treatment for trigger points by Clair Davies with Amber Davies. This book is useful not only for a practitioner to use on his own trigger points and that of his clients, but also as a teaching aid so clients can be taught to participate in their own self-care.

Vibration: Vibration consists of a rocking or gentle shaking of muscle structures or body parts. It is rhythmic and relaxing, and useful for those who cannot tolerate deeper massage strokes. (Vibration can also refer to battery or electrically operated hand-held massage tools.)

Index

About the Author

Shirley Philbrick has owned and operated her own business as a Licensed Massage Therapist in the Northeast for over ten years. Though her foundational training and education is in Swedish massage, she has also acquired additional training or certification in Reiki, aromatherapy, newborn massage, reflexology, trigger point therapy, acupressure, and BodyTalk. Ms. Philbrick specializes in deep relaxation and often combines integrated bodywork with guided meditation in her approach. As a secondary career, Ms. Philbrick is a freelance writer and links to her website, blogs, and other writing ventures can be found at http://about.me/slphilbrick.com.